RECONCILING WAR AND MILITARY TRAUMA

FINDING SAFETY, SECURITY, AND PEACE FROM PTSD THAT ALREADY RESIDE WITHIN YOU!

HARRY SULLIVAN

RECONCILING WAR AND MILITARY TRAUMA

FINDING SAFETY, SECURITY, AND PEACE FROM PTSD THAT ALREADY RESIDE WITHIN YOU!

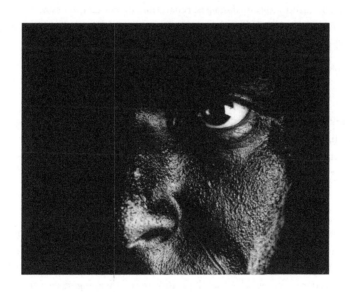

© Copyright 2024 Harry Sullivan. All rights reserved.

The content contained within this book may not be reproduced, duplicated or transmitted without direct written permission from the author or the publisher.

Under no circumstances will any blame or legal responsibility be held against the publisher, or author, for any damages, reparation, or monetary loss due to the information contained within this book, either directly or indirectly. You are responsible for your own choices, actions, and results.

Legal Notice:

This book is copyright protected. This book is for personal use only. You cannot amend, distribute, sell, use, quote or paraphrase any content within this book without the consent of the author or publisher.

Disclaimer Notice:

Please note the information contained within this document is for education and entertainment purposes only. All effort has been executed to present accurate, up to date, reliable, and complete information. No warranties of any kind are declared or implied. Readers acknowledge that the author is not engaging in the rendering of legal, financial, medical or professional advice. The content within this book has been derived from various sources. Please consult a licensed professional before attempting any techniques outlined in this book.

By reading this document, the reader agrees that under no circumstances is the author responsible for any losses, direct or indirect, which are incurred as a result of the use of the information contained within this document, including, but not limited to, — errors, omissions, or inaccuracies.

Just scan the QR code or go to
https://googledocs.com/7 Little Known Ways to Help You Deal
with PTSD Today

To receive a copy of your free ebook
7 Little Known Ways to Help You Deal with PTSD Today

TABLE OF CONTENTS

Introduction	9
Coming Home	23
The Body's Memory	33
Combat Fatigue	47
Getting Help	53
Non-Trauma-Focused Therapies	65
The Family's Role	83
Trusting God Through PTSD	93
Reclaiming Your Life	107
When Wounds Are Reopened—Maintaining Your Recovery	121
Conclusion	129
Appendix I: PTSD Thought Leadership Interviews	133
Appendix II: Additional Resources	139
References	143

DEDICATION

This book is dedicated to my father, who served in World War II as a young man. My father was my biggest hero, and he set an example for me of what it means to be a man.

Growing up, he was always there for each of my siblings and me. He always encouraged us to stick together as a family, yet he let us know that we were each individually unique to him. He never missed a parents' meeting at school and came to every concert. He was very strict, and while I didn't appreciate it then, I am very grateful now for the discipline he instilled in me.

My father was also a praying man. Whenever I rose early enough, I would hear my father praying in his room for us, other family members, and his friends.

Before going to Iraq, I snapped a photo of my father to remember him by, fearing he would not be around when I returned, since he had been diagnosed with cancer. My father said he would wait for me, and he was true to his word. He was hospitalized shortly after I returned home from Iraq. When I went to visit him, he told me he was tired, and the next day, at 89 years old, my father passed away. I am forever grateful that God blessed me with such a great role model.

INTRODUCTION

You may have been through hell, but you don't have to stay there. No matter how often you tell me the war is over, my past is an armor I can't take off.

As I walk into the enormous facility, I realize that the door I enter through is the only way out. The more I go into the structure, the more I realize how much at a disadvantage I'll be in trying to get out safely. And then, as I'm maneuvering around a corridor within the building, I notice barricades and shelves on either side of the passageway that impair my peripheral vision. The sounds of unidentified people behind me, along with a sideways wheeled object blocking the aisle in front of me, further place me in what appears to be a lethal funnel.

My pulse rate increases, and I begin to sweat as I try to move out of this vulnerable posture on to more secure ground. I search for dominant spots to position myself, so that I have my eyes on everyone and my six is secure. To retain maneuverability, I accelerate or decelerate my movements. I am on constant alert until I eventually exit the doorway I entered, and the fresh air and distance give me greater comfort and protection.

Where had I just been? I was not back in the war in Iraq or Afghanistan. Instead, I realized, I'd been in my neighborhood grocery store.

The spiritual and psychological wounds from war are very real, and what I'd just gone through is a natural response to the unusual —and at times traumatic— situations that arise when you serve in a war.

PTSD: A New Name for an Old Problem

Although little research on Post-Traumatic Stress Disorder (PTSD) was conducted before 1980, the condition has existed as long as man. Men, women, and children have been exposed to painful life situations since prehistoric times, with PTSD dogging its victims and their loved ones. Through the ages, doctors, poets, and novelists have written about the effects of trauma. The detrimental effects of such exposure can be found in the works of Shakespeare, Tolstoy, Dickens, and Remarque. Indeed, mentions in literary works date back to Homer's Iliad and Odyssey in the eighth century BC. Historically, however, PTSD symptoms have most closely been associated with combat and war experiences. Perhaps the earliest known case of war-related PTSD occurred in 490 BC when an unhurt Athenian soldier experienced PTSD after seeing his comrade's death. He suffered a case of "hysterical blindness" (Herodotus, 1890).

In the centuries since, PTSD has acquired various names, referred to as "war tiredness," "soldier's heart," and "shell shock." Different wars, different names. Attempts to document and comprehend such occurrences and their repercussions, within a scientific or medical setting, date back to the mid-nineteenth century. For instance, archival compensation and pension statistics from the American Civil War show that high rates of traumatic exposure were related to increased physical and psychological discomfort rates. During World War I, Adolf Hitler would suffer temporary blindness—perhaps not unlike that of the Athenian soldier—while engaged in combat. Hitler was so humiliated by this incident that upon becoming dictator, he banned the term "shell shock" and prohibited Nazi troopers from receiving psychiatric diagnoses.

PTSD, of course, has no prejudice for power, and even high-ranking, highly trained individuals who are thoroughly checked mentally before being assigned to dangerous activities can develop PTSD. Additionally, PTSD is not exclusive to troops. It can manifest itself in citizens of all ages and backgrounds, including those with no prior history of mental illness.

Following World War II, PTSD research accelerated. At that time, academics and clinicians began documenting the psychological anguish of soldiers, prisoners of war, and concentration camp inmates. "Post-Traumatic Stress Disorder" became official with the publication of the third edition of the Diagnostic and Statistical Manual of Mental Health Disorders in 1980. While the diagnosis has changed slightly since then, the symptoms clinically associated with PTSD have remained mostly the same.

A Fulfilling Call to Duty

While military service members and veterans make up a small percentage of the US population, many Americans know or have family members who have served, and their service makes a significant impact on the population at large. We generally adore our military members, a deserving group of individuals who should be afforded all available assistance.

Working with service members and veterans struggling with PTSD, as professionals such as I do, is an incredibly satisfying job, assisting in the healing of a population of individuals who have contributed to protecting our country and our freedom. There is no greater sense of fulfillment. And after 9/11, an increasing number of mental health specialists stepped up to meet the growing demand. This is not an easy task, and combat and operational stress, in particular, pose a substantial dilemma. Recently, more focus has been shined on our military's mental health, resulting in a tremendous and well-deserved surge in resources.

However, a laser-like focus on the issue can have unexpected repercussions: While we need to take essential steps to ensure that service members and veterans receive help with their mental health, we don't want to infer that mental health problems persist all the time. Yet, the George W. Bush Institute did a study in 2016 that found that 40% of Americans think that more than half of post-9/11 veterans have mental health problems. Is it possible that so much attention has been paid to PTSD among veterans and service members that it has created a perception that it is the norm? On the other hand, a sizable segment of society does not believe military service or deployment to a war zone is generally harmful. Go figure. In fact, there may be good days and bad days, good months or years, and bad months or years. Many of us do expect veterans to be shattered and broken as a result of battle exposure or being in a war zone.

As I began writing this book—offering practical assistance, compassion, and encouragement to those coping with PTSD—the twentieth anniversary of 9/11 had passed me by. New terrorist groups had emerged, far more heinous than the previous ones. Security checks and rechecks remain a way of life: remove your shoes and place them in the container; empty your pockets of everything metal; and raise your arms above your head for the X-ray equivalent of a strip search. Military resilience training, comprehensive soldier fitness education, and a focus on post-traumatic growth are among initiatives aimed to keep young service members from getting hurt. Still, thousands and thousands of them have been injured in many different ways through repeated deployments, exposure to guerilla-style warfare, and IED blasts that cause amputations and traumatic brain injuries.

Life seldom goes according to plan for any of us, let alone service members, yet we frequently thrive, doing the best we can in the face of adversity. However, suppose you have been exposed to a potentially life-threatening or traumatic event. Life might suddenly become more complex, and you may find yourself "surviving" rather than living daily. The world can become abruptly unsettling and frightening. You may begin to avoid circumstances that bring up memories of your trauma. The World Mental Health Survey, which surveyed 70,000 people from 24 countries, discovered that 70% of respondents had experienced at least one stressful event, and we all have almost certainly interacted with one of those individuals who might have been through a horrific event. However, we may be unaware of this information about them because trauma is not a topic of daily discourse.

Take Heart in the Possibility of Recovery

If you're that person, trying to rise above trauma, whatever stage of recovery you are currently at, there is always room for improvement. If you feel as though you've been trapped in an endless cycle of struggle and pain, take heart. There is another route, a more hopeful one for you. There is a path that has been demonstrated to have successfully assisted individuals in achieving a healthier, happier existence. And this book will point you in the direction toward that path. This guide will provide you with time-tested and well-researched ways of learning to go forward, while enhancing your well-being and quality of life, though there is no correct or incorrect method for completing the exercises within.

There is also no completion date specified. Allow yourself numerous opportunities to go over this guide. Connect with your thoughts and feelings, and your prior recollections will gradually become less frightening. Please permit me to accompany you as a guide on your journey toward what is known as "post-traumatic development." I have witnessed individuals heal. You, too, are capable of healing. I'm going to walk with you on this PTSD journey by presenting you with the same well-researched and proven therapeutic techniques that I experienced myself so that you can thrive as well.

This publication's principles are based on the most successful trauma recovery therapies. By addressing complex wounds from your past, you will develop the skills necessary to improve your physical and mental health by addressing them without feeling overwhelmed by emotions. My objective is to assist you in discovering a new sense of liberation. Your past traumatic events should no longer impair your ability to live a meaningful and satisfying life.

This book is particularly written to assist those of you who are still suffering from terrible flashbacks, memories, and feelings resulting from a traumatic experience. Up to 90% of us will be exposed to a traumatic experience during our lifetimes. Some of us will continue to struggle with these experiences in ways that haunt us, impair our well-being, and make it difficult to go on with our lives. Although this is a self-help book, I recommend to anyone struggling with PTSD to also seek the assistance of a therapist to aid in the recovery process. If your symptoms have been going on

INTRODUCTION | 15

for a long time and are affecting your quality of life or stopping you from doing the things you enjoy, you may need professional help beyond these pages.

This guide, however, can help you learn how to cultivate and apply self-compassion to examine the impact of traumatic experiences on ideas, emotions, motivations, and behaviors; it also discusses some helpful coping mechanisms. If you think this is easy or, instead, that you do not deserve compassion (which is not as uncommon as you might believe), the truth is that compassion can be a complicated strategy to adopt since it requires you to be willing to confront the things that upset and disturb your state of being. Compassion aids in this process and may feel taxing but not overpowering.

> *If you don't speak up, you don't get noticed. If you don't get noticed, you don't get help. If you don't get help, you're left to rot. If you're left to rot, you die.*
>
> — ANTHONY LOCKE

This is not a treatment manual for PTSD, nor is it an attempt to cure it. Neither is it a guidebook for marriage or relationships. The objective of this manual is to offer compassion, encouragement, and practical assistance to you—the service member or veteran—and spouses, families, and other loved ones of soldiers who have been diagnosed with PTSD. Their golden hearts drew us to them, and our lives have been devoted to loving them. The more veterans' families I meet, the more I realize that those who are drawn to help them also have golden hearts. I'm curious if sorrow is the catalyst that transforms hearts into gold.

This is a straightforward book—so real, so genuine. You may see yourself in it, and I'm guessing your tale may be very similar to mine and that we have a great deal in common. Do you wonder how perplexing it is that no one else seems to get it? We battle fear, isolation, worry, and restless nights. We doubt our sanity and undergo monthly hormone screenings to determine levels of medication effectiveness. We are afraid to admit to anyone that we wonder if we made a mistake with our lives. And, we feel humiliated when brief thoughts occur to us of how much easier life would be without PTSD.

You are not alone in any of this. You share this trip with many individuals, each of whom has some contact with other veterans. Yet you'll notice that the personal experiences originate from a diverse group of people, including me. Although the names may be changed, the accounts are genuine. Many of us have frequently considered quitting—and a few have—but many more are becoming stronger every day, not despite PTSD but because of PTSD. The faith and love that have prevented us from collapsing, also sustain, console and strengthen us, and that faith and love is available to all of us. We need one another. Through sharing our problems and successes, our suffering and healing, our tears and happiness, we learn to love the service members and veterans among us even more. For those of you who are struggling to love that individual with PTSD, I am writing this book hoping that it will give you hope and inspiration.

According to the U.S. Department of Veterans Affairs, eleven to twenty veterans out of every hundred who have seen combat are now estimated to have complicated PTSD. This means that almost 20% of our military families suffer, since warriors are not usually suffering in isolation. PTSD throws an entire household into disarray. While there are an endless number of brave spouses, parents, children, and friends who have pledged to love their veteran through it all—with all their hearts and souls—remember that if you're that veteran, you're just as important to them as they are to you. This manuscript will give everyone in this equation excellent insight into how a warrior's unseen wounds can negatively affect veterans and those close to them. Most importantly, the material will show that disorders such as PTSD, depression, and anxiety can be treated. Service members can develop coping skills for everyday life and find true peace after war!

To my fellow service members: You have borne an excruciating responsibility for this country that only you and those who fought beside you fully comprehend. Maybe you can relate to this soldier's thoughts:

> *I bear responsibility. They died. Close my eyes, and I'll still see their faces. I'm not a hero; I'm a monster. If you only knew, where was God? Is he punishing me?*
>
> — A SOLDIER ON ACTIVE DUTY

This erroneous view of the world might create difficulties in social and professional settings and wreak havoc on relationships with family, friends, neighbors, and coworkers. Yet, if you have PTSD, you too may encounter these types of intrusive memories and flashbacks to horrific events. In this manuscript, I will chronicle the difficulties I also encountered during my military career, including the anguish of losing a close friend and my experiences and challenges when I left the service.

On that note, let me explain why I thought this guide needed to be written. To begin with, like veterans of previous wars who shared their experiences for posterity, I am writing this to ensure that the sacrifices made by warriors deployed in recent conflicts are not forgotten. While being in the military is our common ground, our stories are all unique. I can benefit from hearing your story, and I hope you benefit from mine.

While there are numerous PTSD resources available, I've also noticed that many of them are authored by individuals who have never been on the front lines. I believe they have the best intentions, but many military personnel and first responders struggle to relate to PTSD counselors who have never been there. As the adage goes, it takes one to know one. Can someone entirely comprehend what you've gone through unless they are familiar with the sights, sounds, and smells? That's why I advise you to be resolute when choosing a provider. If the provider isn't the right fit for you, request or seek another one. A plaque or certificate on someone's wall does not make them a competent or skilled provider. However, that being said, no topic I discuss in this book is a substitute for competent mental health counseling.

I also want to be clear that even if someone has not served in the military, it does not mean their commitment to serving our veterans is lacking and, in fact, it can be just as strong. As an example: Prior to my retiring from a VA medical center (VAMC), my usual shift was 7:30 a.m.-8:00 p.m. Most social worker shifts ended at 4:00 p.m.—at which point some of them couldn't leave fast enough, or I'd hear them say, "I'm off," hightailing it out the exits at 3:45 p.m. Then there was a new social worker I'd see still tending to patients at 8:00 p.m., as I was leaving. She was dedicated to serving our veterans, no matter that her shift had ended, and she was no longer being paid. There are countless others like her, incredibly dedicated to their VAMC jobs though not veterans themselves.

We all need to believe and trust in someone that can help us, whoever that person might be—or whatever high power it might be.

> *He who dwells in the shelter of the Highest will abide in the shadow of the Almighty. I will say to the LORD, "He is my refuge and my fortress, my God, in whom I trust."*
>
> — PSALM 91:1-2

Rest assured that you among our troops who give their lives in the service of others—often in distant lands among distant peoples—are heroes we never want to forget. We thank God that such exceptional human beings exist and, like angels, protect our way of life.

> *Yea, though I walk through the valley of the shadow of death, I will fear no evil; for thou art with me; thy rod and thy staff comfort me.*
>
> — PSALM 23:4

> *To have a shadow, you have to have light. Jesus is the light.*
>
> — JOHN 8:12

Again, the pages that follow are designed to assist you, among our heroes, in coping healthily and productively with the consequences of traumatic incidents. You'll learn more about PTSD, how it develops, and how to lead a happier life. The past (up to this point) cannot be altered or reversed. What may be altered is your perception of and response to what has occurred to you.

This guide will educate you on trauma and PTSD, introduce you to new concepts, and provide strategies to help you overcome your PTSD. Each part and activity within is designed to assist you in reclaiming your life. When you close this guide, however, you are not closing PTSD. Trauma rehabilitation is a lifelong journey, and there will almost certainly be periods when you feel as though you've again lost control of your PTSD. My intention is to equip you so that you can allow yourself opportunities to truly reflect on your trauma and PTSD to heal and recover.

You, however, will retain all authority and control over the strategies contained in this guidebook. Your focus will determine your destination. Change your focus and you can change your destination. By the end of this book, I hope you'll see that your trauma does not define who you are as a person and that the work you've done in these pages has transformed you into a more capable, resilient, and better survivor.

To recover from developmental trauma, you must have a "reparative connection experience." This means that you welcome sensations of bewilderment, discomfort, rage, sadness, shame, and pain inside the space of another. In this case, it should be a loving therapist—again, one that is chosen carefully. Utilizing this guide in conjunction with psychotherapy can educate and deepen understanding, hence reducing treatment time and cost. A sympathetic therapist acts as a container for the emotions and memories that you may be unable to manage on your own. And together, you'll develop trust, acquire perspective, and discover the most effective healing strategies that work for you. The words in this manuscript will assist you further in accessing the healing force that resides within you.

Without a doubt, there will be anguish and sorrow on this journey. On the other hand, self-awareness provides the keys to empowerment and personal independence. Non-stigmatizing and strength-based approaches to recovery are found across these pages. You are not broken and in desperate need of repair. Rather, you are profoundly hurt and in need of assistance. With enough assistance, you will be able to let go of your defensive self-protection and unveil your inherent worth, wisdom, and creativity —in other words, your greatness.

While I am a professional in mental health with twenty-plus years of experience and am well-versed in death, grieving, and mental health, I'm made errors in my own personal life when dealing with PTSD myself. I'm also presenting these issues hoping that, among other things, you can learn from my errors and avoid repeating them in your own life or having those issues negatively impact those you care about. I want you to uncover your resiliency, as have I.

Your personal starting point begins with that fact that your past has formed your present, distinct viewpoint on what it means to be alive. Now, only you have the authority to decide what to do with your life at this moment, but if you're reading this, you are on the right course. You've arrived. You are a trauma survivor. You have overcome adversity. Now let us work together to overcome PTSD. Allow the words that follow assist you in dismantling your agonizing beliefs so that you can finally feel serenity. You are not alone in this journey.

COMING HOME

YOU ARE TRAINED TO BE A SOLDIER, A KILLER, BUT YOU ARE NOT TRAINED TO BE A CIVILIAN AGAIN.

ALL MY LIFE, I've been a fighter. I went into the military immediately after graduating high school. I was a boxer. As a fighter, I had 225 amateur fights. I was a pretty good boxer, winning many championships. I was a two-time, Light-

Heavyweight Golden Glove Champion 1981 and 1982, for both city and district in Cleveland, Ohio. I won the All-Navy Light-Heavyweight Championship in 1983 and the All-Marine Corps Light-Heavyweight Championship in 1984. By doing that, I set a military record, becoming the first person in military history to win back-to-back titles in two different services. After several years of not fighting, I came back in 1990. In 1992, I won a silver medal in the US championships, followed by a 1994 win of the Southeast Regionals in the US, which was also my last fight. My record was 212 wins with 13 losses, and I won more than 150 of my fights by KO.

I am a registered nurse, having worked in the medical field for twenty-five years, which included caring for people with PTSD—before I went to Iraq and experienced PTSD myself. I admit, I didn't fully understand PTSD pre-Iraq. When people were telling their stories, I was sympathetic toward them but couldn't fully understand what they were going through. As medical professionals, we have the training to help those with PTSD. Still, without firsthand experience, we don't totally understand what PTSD patients are going through. There are exceptions, of course, and I have come across very committed and effective therapists without any personal history of PTSD, so a therapist's personal experience is not a deal-breaker. A PTSD patient often doesn't care how much you know—if they know how much you care.

More than 90% of the patients I came across drank obsessively, used street drugs, or had suicidal tendencies. However, alcoholism, drugs, or suicidal tendencies were not the main problems. They were symptoms of the main problem—PTSD! They were drinking or using drugs, not because they were addicted. But, because they were trying to drown out the voices in their heads, the intrusive thoughts, and the nightmares they experienced due to their trauma.

How has PTSD affected my own daily life? Let me give you a small example. I was taking my adult son Dave to Walmart one late night. As soon as we entered the store, the bright lights hit me, and it felt like I was back on base in Iraq with the spotlights glaring.

"We have to go!" I blurted to Dave, ushering him out. I didn't tell him why we were leaving in a hurry. We just had to go—and now.

Back at his house, after saying goodnight to him, it took me nearly an hour to calm myself. A week later, I shared the incident during my counseling session. "How did your son feel about it?" the counselor asked. It's then that I realized my son must have felt he'd done something wrong, but my anxiety had been so high at the time, I couldn't organize my thoughts enough to tell him about the havoc in my head. Sound familiar? After that session, I immediately called my son and explained the situation, and he was appreciative!

When I was first deployed to Iraq in 2010, the experience changed me. I was the Chief Patient Administrator for a Task Force Combat Support Hospital (CSH) in the hotspot of Tikrit—Saddam's hometown. My job was to manage the flow of patients, including incoming mass casualties (MASCAL) and the evacuation of US casualties; I would track them until they reached a level five medical center in the states or returned to their units. I didn't just handle the flow of US military personnel—but injured civilians and enemies alike. We had two other CSH's and clinics as well, further afield. When I'd arrived to take on my responsibilities, however, I'd been hit with a bomb, figuratively, when I was handed a tertiary job—that of mortuary affairs officer for the base. This was PTSD in the making.

A sad fact was that in Iraq, most of the soldiers I was putting in body bags were younger than my own children, and it was always hard for me to shake the analogy. I just couldn't imagine how the parents of these soldiers would feel when retrieving their child's body. Instead of dreams that their sons would marry, start families, have children, and the parents could play with their grandchildren, instead, they had to deal with the death of their young sons or daughters. It was a very emotional role I had, but one that I took on with the greatest dignity humanely possible.

During this deployment, my main concern was not about myself but that of my fellow soldiers' well-being under my supervision. My responsibility was to make sure that they were safe, not put in harm's way unnecessarily, and got home safely. We faced some tough times.

While on base one morning my wife (at the time) called and told me she was divorcing me. The news was totally unexpected. After the call, I went to eat breakfast, not wanting to talk to anyone because I needed to deal with this news. As I was eating, a close friend of mine, a major, approached me. He looked very distressed and was shaking like a leaf. He was holding his breakfast tray, and it was shaking too. I understood something significant was going on, but I needed to deal with my own problem at that moment. As my friend put his tray on the table, I picked mine up to leave and told him I would talk to him later. I looked at him, and he looked despondent, but I had my issues and needed some alone time. It's the last time I would seem him alive.

I was in my office a few hours later when someone knocked on my door and exclaimed, "Captain, you need to come to the latrines now! Someone committed suicide!"

I ran to the latrines, asking as I arrived the dreaded question, "Who?" As soon as I heard the name of my close friend, the whole world around me stopped. I lost all my strength and fell to the ground. I don't know how long I was on the ground. Finally, I was able to gather myself and go into the latrines. We couldn't move my friend's body right away because the Army's Criminal Investigation Division (CID) needed to do its investigation.

After CID did its thing, we took my friend's body to an Angel Tent, where I spent a few hours beside his body before he would be taken to the morgue. I kept thinking, "What if I talked to him this morning instead of avoiding him? . . . He could still be alive. Am I in any way responsible for his death?"

We had been in the unit together a long time. My mind flashed back to right before our deployment, when we had spent a weekend in Washington, DC together, running in the Army Ten-Miler. Then during our flight to Iraq soon after, he asked for my phone and took a picture of me. In return, I took a picture of him with the biggest smile on his face. That smile was etched in my mind in the midst of this now unbearable time, when before me was a very different picture of my friend that would continue to haunt me for years to come.

Upon returning home later the same year, I didn't feel much different though others noticed changes---like my sister, who had deployed to Iraq four years earlier as a nurse in a similar combat support hospital. Within two weeks of my coming back home, she told me, "Harry, you need to get help!"

But warrior that I was, I didn't seek help until the following year, in 2012, and at that point, I was given medications that made me sleep but didn't do anything for my mental state. Not much about my PTSD changed.

Two years later, in my Army Reserves unit in Ohio, I became commander of a small unit in our battalion and was very busy with soldiers under my command—so busy that I didn't experience many symptoms of PTSD. Things grew worse, however, and in 2015, the stress and anxiety from symptoms related to PTSD caused me to have a heart attack while at Battle Assembly with my unit. An ambulance sped me to the hospital, and I was admitted, but I didn't share with anyone what I was mentally dealing with. However, when I was later rotated out of command and was back in a Patient Admin division position in Ohio, things got worse. I had plenty of downtime, and the PTSD hit me.

The bad memories of the war and the nightmares gradually started overwhelming me. "An idle mind is the devil's workshop." I started to experience aggressive PTSD symptoms. For one five-day period, I couldn't sleep because as soon as I closed my eyes, the memories of my friend who died in Iraq flooded me. The situation was so bad that I didn't want to get out of bed or leave my bedroom. My wife would bring me food, but I wasn't interested in eating. While I was physically back in the United States and in my house, mentally I was still in Iraq. It was a living hell, and I was fighting my demons. To tell you the truth, I was even contemplating thoughts of committing suicide.

I later was in training in Fort McCoy, Wisconsin, when an assigned first sergeant came up the steps of the bus I was on. He looked just like my buddy who committed suicide, and as the first sergeant looked at me, it felt as if I was seeing my long-lost friend. That night, I was back in the barracks trying to sleep, but after seeing that ghost, the nightmares and horrible memories of my war experience resurfaced in my mind.

When you're in a war, you are always on alert, and when you return home, it's hard to turn off those feelings of alertness. So at home I had bought an M-4 and kept it with me—the same type assigned to me in Iraq, which was initially an M-4, then a 9mm. It gave me comfort and made me feel secure, and I also always kept an extra round (5.56mm) in my pocket just in case I decided to end my life.

Now, at Fort McCoy besides my bed, one of my fellow soldiers had his service M-4 next to him. I kept thinking that I should take the M-4, go to the bathroom, and end my miserable life once and for all!

But then, God spoke to me. God told me to talk to a buddy, whom I had known since 2005 when I first joined the unit. He was a sergeant back then, but later became an RN and commissioned, got his Master's, and was now a nurse practitioner in my unit. So I went to him, told him what was going on, and he took me to the medical center on Fort McCoy (Thank you, Mateosky). There I got referred for follow-up PTSD treatment. Initially, I was assigned a therapist who provided more of the same old-same old textbook treatment that I'd received since first being diagnosed with PTSD years earlier.

At work in the meantime, I was struggling as a nurse in the Acute Mental Health Unit especially in the treatment team meetings for our patients. I would outwardly keep my composure, but inside I was breaking down listening to veterans' stories of what they endured in Iraq and Afghanistan. When I was experiencing anxiety, I would often lock myself in the bathroom at work, thinking no one noticed. But one day someone did—the person I thought disliked me most in the unit. She checked up on me, asking if I was OK. It was another God-awakening moment for me, having that one person show true concern for me when I was very much in need of it.

Another awakening moment for me was when my wife questioned whether I was happy with her, because she felt that no matter what she did, I seemed unhappy or depressed. Yes, I was depressed, and my emotional state on a scale of 0-10—with 0 being low and 10 being high—was constantly at 0. I heard that the PTSD treatment program at Fort Thomas, Kentucky was one of if not the best in the country. I approached the Operation Iraqi Freedom/Operation Enduring Freedom (OIF/OEF) Liaison personnel, Melissa, when she was making rounds in our unit at the VA Hospital, and she got me signed up for the seven-week residential treatment program at Fort Thomas.

That was a turning point for me. It was there that I was able to replace the memory of my friend from that of him in the Angel Tent to the smiling-face picture of him in that special moment we shared on the plane deploying to Iraq. I realized that God knows all things. That is why he allowed me to take that picture, so a happy memory of my friend stays with me. During that treatment, I understood that even if I had talked to him that morning, it might not have changed the outcome. His death was not my fault. I did much for my friend—including helping prepare with dignity for his body to be sent home.

The seven-week program helped me overcome my major symptoms of PTSD, with my suicidal tendencies gone, and I was not living the nightmares of war as often. I received behavioral processing therapy, cognitive processing therapy, and exposure therapy. These are evidence-based therapies proven to work. And, I had an effective therapist who also helped me deal with my "stuck points"—events that kept me paralyzed in the trauma of war, like the glaring lights of Walmart. Stuck points keep you from moving forward by relying on false truths that you tell yourself. But no longer. I was on the road to recovery.

One year later, I went to a free weekend retreat that a fellow soldier deployed to Iraq had told me about. Called HOOVES

(Healing Of Our Veterans through Equine Services), it was equine-assisted facilitation for PTSD, and though the retreat was only four days, it was amazingly effective.

I have since retired from both the military and the VA. So now I want to give back. While I previously noted my "why" for writing this book—to help my fellow brothers and sisters going through similar experiences with PTSD—I am not limiting myself to a book on PTSD recovery. I plan to build a place called "The Farm" for people with PTSD, establishing it in my home base of Ohio as a non-profit organization. My goal is to have The Farm a safe haven where veterans can get back to normality after returning from war. It will be a similarly minded community where veterans can be amongst themselves, helping each other to overcome the traumas of war. A place to retreat, recover, and even retire. I plan to have services (to be determined) to help veterans cope with PTSD and other issues common to our community. And I'd like to set in motion ways for those at The Farm to serve the community and our country. It is important for people to have a purpose or they risk declining and fading away.

Having seen the horrors of war firsthand—and suffered from PTSD and received help, I know that I am in a position to help other soldiers suffering from PTSD. I might also add that while a lot of veterans are scared to talk about their PTSD because of the culture, dealing with PTSD has nothing to do with weakness or strength. We were taught a course both while in Iraq and at home known as "Master Resiliency Training" (MRT). I was an MRT trainer. The course taught us that prolonged exposure to war would cause you to develop PTSD no matter whether you are weak or strong.

And that is a critical point I hope to relay to both active-duty military personnel and veterans: PTSD is a common occurrence under traumatic or prolonged stressful situations. Just like when it is raining, if you go outside you will get wet; If you are deployed in war zones, you will likely suffer from PTSD. It is a normal occurrence.

So let's move on to working to get better.

THE BODY'S MEMORY

WHEN WAS the first time you heard the sound of a gun going off? The first time a close friend was killed by a gunshot? How did you feel the first time you stepped foot in a conflict zone? No matter how long ago these situations might have occurred, they will typically elicit sentiments that the body remembers. It is called "trauma imprinting"—a term used to describe the psychological effects of traumatic events. Individuals' minds and bodies are imprinted with traumatic experiences at the moment they first feel startled, stunned, or terrified. This imprint is phobic in that the learning happens immediately after the first shock. Until the trauma imprint is deliberately removed by procedures that remove phobias, the imprint is frozen in the body and can cause "flashbacks" when the body is exposed to certain triggers.

KNOWING YOUR BODY AND YOUR MIND: A GUIDE TO TRAUMA

To understand how the brain and body respond to trauma, it's necessary to understand various regions of the brain. The limbic system that processes emotions and memories includes the hippocampus, amygdala, hypothalamus, thalamus, cingulate cortex, basal ganglia, dentate gyrus, parahippocampal gyrus, subiculum, and the mammillary body located in the center of the brain. The amygdala, within this limbic system, is activated when a person experiences a traumatic incident, and the memory is stored there. The amygdala stores the emotional significance of an event, as well as the strength and force of the emotion that caused it.

On a roller coaster, for example, your sensory information includes fear, speed, stress, and thrill, but none of them in life-threatening forms. Because it's a three-minute ride, the amygdala can deduce the emotional impact of the event, with the visual impressions of trauma retained as sensory fragments—not stored as a permanent tale but rather by how our five senses temporarily perceive information at the time it was occurring. Among the five senses, visual, auditory, and gustatory (taste) memories can all be accessed through the sense of touch due to tactile stimuli in each of those three areas—visual, auditory, and gustatory. For example the mouth, more specifically the tongue, and the hands have the most tactile receptors in the body.

After a traumatic event, however, the brain can be quickly triggered by sensory input, interpreting typical situations as dangerous rather than innocuous like the roller-coaster ride. A red light, for example, is no longer a red light but rather a potential spark. The sound of a BBQ could be mistaken for an explosion.

Misinterpretation of sensory pieces causes the brain to lose the ability to distinguish between what is dangerous and what is normal. This occurs in the section of the brain called the prefrontal cortex, where consciousness and reasoning take place. This section also makes sense of language. This prefrontal cortex, however, may shut down in response to a traumatic event that prompts "fight, flight, or freeze" reactions. Disorganized and overloaded due to emotional or physical trauma, the brain is put into a survival mode and is unable to process information. A deeply imprinted stress response occurs as a result of the metabolic shutdown.

HOW DOES THE BODY STORE UNPROCESSED TRAUMA?

Our brains are the most powerful computers on the planet—when everything is running smoothly. In addition to being extremely efficient in processing and organizing information, the brain's vast network of around 100 billion neurons is also extremely rapid. As many as 640 trillion electrical pulses are coursing through your brain every second. In this matrix, everything you've ever done and thought about is meticulously coded and stored. This makes up the mosaic of you.

However, what happens when the system is thrown off course by an unexpected event? And why is it that a person's health might be negatively impacted for years after a traumatic event? True trauma doesn't just happen in your thoughts. Your memory storage mechanisms are disrupted, and your brain alters as a result.

This is why past trauma can have a long-term effect on your health if you don't deal with it. The stress can increase risks of heart attack, stroke, weight gain, and cancer due to the mental and physical reactions it causes, according to Harvard Medical School studies.

In addition, the number of traumatic incidents endured raises the likelihood of mental and physical health problems. This phenomenon was noted in a study of repeat traumas in children, by Harvard research scientist Andrea Roberts. Points out Roberts, "Your risk for issues is substantially larger if you've experienced three or more unfavorable events, called adverse childhood experiences (ACE)."

An unseen wound can impair the body's defenses, causing an illness even if the trauma survivor appears well. What then occurs when we are subjected to trauma? And where does the body store it? If our supercomputer gets jolted by an external force, the declarative-explicit memory system, which is activated by trauma, doesn't work properly. Traumatic memories may not be properly recorded and kept. Our supercomputer instead uses the memory system to record signals, imprinting traumatizing memories in the form of images or physical sensations. Memories become fragmented in a condition known as dissociation. Like shrapnel, they remain lodged deep within the mind, preventing the brain's normal recovery process. Malicious fragments may appear as signs of PTSD and raise our chance of developing major health problems. PTSD affects the brain in a noticeable way.

In 2017, an attack on Ariana Grande's concert in Manchester, England, killed twenty-two people, and a brain scan done on the singer revealed the extent of the damage done to her brain as a result of the attack. She talked about her PTSD and said, "When I think about my own experiences, I feel like I should not even be talking about them. Even if I could talk about it without crying, I don't know how. So many individuals have lost so much, and it's difficult to talk about it. It's a real thing."

Changes in the three areas of the brain that deal with stress may be seen in those who suffer from PTSD.

- The hippocampus, the brain's emotional and memory center, declines with age.
- The amygdala's creative and rumination functions are enhanced.
- The prefrontal/anterior cingulate function, which is in charge of more complicated tasks like planning and self-development, gets less efficient.

Unprocessed trauma may wreak havoc on our brains and bodies in the same way a virus does on our coding system. In fact, early evidence suggests that our bodies' cells may also be able to store painful memories. Maybe that's why a PTSD sufferer may feel emotional pain all over.

IS THERE ANYTHING THAT CAN BE DONE ABOUT THIS "ACTUAL THING?"

The good news is that you don't have to live with the effects of your past traumas. It's a treatable condition, and there are resources available to help. Unlocking or processing traumatic memories in therapy can help free them from your system and allow you to go on with your life. The brain might begin to heal when the painful memory is reintegrated into the mind.

It can begin the healing process if you meditate and do physical activities like yoga, which have been shown to help. In fact, yoga was revealed to be more helpful than any medication evaluated to date in the treatment of PTSD. Although yoga does not cure PTSD, it has a significant positive impact in the right direction.

Releasing one's body and psyche from the effects of trauma can have far-reaching effects. You don't have to be stuck, and there is a strong probability that you can get through this. As fascinating as the human condition is, the human body is the most fascinating structure. Helen Keller, who was deaf and blind, said, "While the world is full of pain, it is also full of those who have overcome it."

GEORGE WASHINGTON AND PTSD

George Washington was a spiritual man, keeping a prayer journal with him in which he wrote thoughts every day. Washington also created the chaplain core in the US military. He knew that war was terrible and that his soldiers might stray from the moral path or be deeply traumatized by the effects of war. So one of his first acts as commander-in-chief was to appoint chaplains to provide mental solace to his soldiers.

Among the first US Army chaplains was William Emerson, who coincidentally was the grandfather of the great philosopher, Ralph Waldo Emerson. William Emerson was at Lexington as the Revolution started to unfold, and it was shortly after that when George Washington named him chaplain. Washington had written to his commanders, "The blessings and protections of heaven are always necessary, but especially so at the time of passion and distress."

We know that Washington pleaded with the Continental Congress during the war for adequate supplies and resources for his soldiers. At war's end, he told a few fellow soldiers who fought beside him during the duration of the war, "Go and live in the woods because you are no longer fit to live in society. War has changed you, and society will not accept you as a normal person." That comment was telling, illustrating how war might change people and isolate them for good.

When Washington became president, he fought to pass bills that guaranteed pension and disability allowances for soldiers who had fought under him. He stayed loyal to his troops, but Congress never approved his requests.

Why am I sharing this history? Because undoubtedly, George Washington witnessed the effects of PTSD firsthand. One of the ways you can survive PTSD is by remembering role models who have experienced it and survived it. Previously, Washington was a young officer during the French and Indian War when he lost his first four battles, and his biographers tell us that Washington remembered the screams of several injured and dying soldiers during those battles. He experienced the horrors of PTSD in some form and was able to survive it. So can you! Think of a commander or mentor you greatly admire who, too, went through horrific war experiences but went on to great things. It's possible!

Personally, I was inspired by reading George Washington's postwar speech to his troops, which is what led me to decide to establish the veterans' Farm that is my goal. But before I can invite you there, let me share some of what I've learned about our reaction to stress:

THE FOUR FORMS OF TRAUMA RESPONSE: FIGHT, FLIGHT, FREEZE, AND FAWN

Stress can benefit short-term conditions, which isn't necessarily bad. Because of this, it can be taxing and detrimental to the body in times after the crisis event has passed. Here's the forms that stress may take:

The fighting response

When the fight response is functioning properly, it can be used to assert yourself and set clear limits. During a traumatic event, your body's natural response is to move toward conflict with anger and hatred in order to protect yourself. This is the first element of what is called "fight or flight." It's a condition of apprehension in which you face the possibility of having to speak up for yourself. Conflict is a tool that people use to get through difficult situations. While the threat is able to maintain its hold, in the fight response you try to achieve control. When this happens, it might take the form of physical fighting, yelling, physical aggression, hurling objects, or even damage to property. Some examples include making fists out of your hands, feeling like you're about to burst into tears, or having an extremely tense jaw.

If the fight response is your reaction to stress, assuming you're not in a dangerous situation, stop what you're doing and take a moment to reflect on where you're currently positioned in relation to the people around you. To gain mobility and make your inner self match the outside world, you have to focus on your physical well-being. You'll have tunnel vision, focused on yourself rather than those around you. The fight reaction prepares you to be physically active, so you can also engage in physical activity to bring your body back to a state of equilibrium. Deep breathing, self-awareness, routines, a warm bath afterwards, and being kind to yourself can all help you relieve tension. The parasympathetic nervous system is activated when you engage in a short burst of physical activity, like yoga or stretching, and it can take the edge off and helps you reconnect with your surroundings.

The flight response

It's common for people to flee when confronted with perilous situations. When you're in good health, you can detect and disengage from stressful situations and that may mean choosing flight to avoid conflict and hurt, including evading individuals, avoiding social situations, or heading for the exit sign. You can also avoid unpleasant feelings by staying busy when things get difficult. If you're experiencing trauma, you may go so far as isolating yourself completely.

With this type of stress response, to return to your true self, undertake actions that elicit an immediate, visceral response from your body. Relax any muscles that are tense, and your mind will follow suit. Using bodywork and deliberate motions to delay the stress response can allow you to think about your desired response rather than your first instinct, experts say. Drinking a hot beverage or munching on a piece of crunchy food can help alleviate stress. As a result, feel-good hormones like endorphins and serotonin are released into the body, making you happier.

The freeze response

Slowing down and taking your time to assess the issue is one of the benefits of having a good freeze response. Unhealthy freeze responses are linked to dissociation and immobility. As a result of this protection, you may find yourself in a state of "freezing"— unable to move or apathetic, as though you were in a haze or disconnected from reality. As a means of ensuring your emotional well-being, it is common to get disengaged from your surroundings and forget about what is going on around you. Your sympathetic nervous system reaches a point of exhaustion, resulting in a "frozen trauma reaction." Consider how our animal buddies react when confronted by a predator. You could be unable to express yourself, have difficulty breaking out of your mental cocoon, sleep, dissociate or space out, and become emotionally or physically numb when you freeze. It's akin to being temporarily paralyzed and removing yourself from your body to avoid further stress. Grounding exercises might help you get your sense of self-awareness back if you start to forget about reality.

The fawn response

When it comes to fawning, it's all about making other people happy. By doing anything they desire in order for you to gain favor, it prioritizes individuals above all else. It may seem to be a good idea to be well-liked and to defer to others to ensure your safety, but not if it comes at the expense of your own identity. It's possible to lose sight of who you are and what you need when you become so entwined with others. Most likely, you don't get the attention you deserve and may feel like you're being overshadowed by your friends and family. Fawn responses are so self-oblivious to the surroundings that you lose all sense of your own thoughts and feelings. In the beginning stages of separating your own feelings from those of others, be extra kind to yourself if you notice yourself fawning frequently. To avoid fawning, observe yourself when you're around people to add buffering time. The first stage is to become conscious and learn how to set boundaries in order to claim a certain amount of space.

Moving on from the types of responses to stress are the imprints that are left from the stressors. There is a basic structure to how trauma and loss leave their imprints—whether from the loss of a loved one (Loss Trauma Imprint) or a violent attack (Violence Trauma Imprint):

LOSS TRAUMA IMPRINT

Initial Shock: When you first notice that something is wrong, you may experience an initial sense of disbelief/denial. Fear-induced adrenaline rushes are common when a person experiences a shock. Popular responses are, "I don't believe it," or "It's not true."

Limiting Core Beliefs: Responsibility (guilt/shame/blame)

- A loss is difficult to comprehend, and those who experience it strive to make sense of it. You may come to the erroneous conclusion that the loss is your responsibility in some way, feeling guilty or ashamed, and so on.
- "Whose responsibility is it to look after me?" After the death of a family member or friend who was part of your support network, the loss may cause you to worry about who will take care of your physical, emotional, and social needs.
- "There are a lot of people who leave me. I'm not going to put my faith in them." This viewpoint can occur in a variety of settings. It shows up as a dread of making new acquaintances as well as behavior that results in friendships being broken apart.
- "I'm undesirable, unappreciated, and unworthy." The idea that "I am worthless" may create behaviors that make you wary of those who show an interest in you. In order to get the affection, friendship, and attention of others, you often resort to "bribing" them by taking care of them, doing

something nice for them, or attempting to transform yourself into what you believe the other person wants.
- Feeling of Emptiness. When you lose a loved one, you naturally miss them. Emptiness or hollowness can be felt in the stomach and chest as a result of the loss. Some people develop food addictions to deal with the emptiness caused by rejection or loss.

If you've lost someone you care about, you're probably afraid that you'll lose someone else you care about. Whether experiencing that type of loss or the violent traumas addressed below, "anticipatory phobia" can result. Many basic trauma imprints share this anticipatory phobia, which is a dread and deep sense of foreboding that the trauma will happen again.

VIOLENCE TRAUMA IMPRINT

Initial Shock: The initial sensation of shock or fear permeates every layer of your being, all at the same time. This occurs as a result of a) physical or verbal violence; b) anger/rage; c) sadness, and; d) hurt/pain imprinted on the body. Both physical and emotional harm are possible outcomes of physical aggression.

Limiting Core Beliefs: Reactions and Responsibility (guilt/shame/blame)

- Similar to a "loss imprint," violence trauma leaves an indelible mark on your mind. You may attempt to justify the perpetrator's actions.
- You may feel certain that you are somehow responsible for the attack. Oft-heard admonitions include, "I should have known better" and "I should not have dressed like that."
- It's not uncommon to point the finger at everyone but the attacker.

- "God should really have shielded me" is added to the list of beliefs about God and religion in a violence/loss trauma imprint.

Added to the above Loss Trauma Imprint and Violence Trauma Imprint is the loss imprint from being subjected to violence with a "Root Cause Unknown." Random violence or mayhem can be the cause in those instances, such as being a victim in the random bombing of a building by an as-yet unidentified perpetrator.

COMBAT FATIGUE

WHAT IS PTSD?

TRAUMATIC EVENTS such as natural disasters, catastrophic accidents, terrorist acts, war, combat, and rape are among the many possible causes for PTSD. PTSD stems from situations where there is surprise/unpreparedness and then insufficient resilience of coping strategy to process the event(s). Earlier eras had different names for it, "shell shock" during World War I and "battle exhaustion" during World War II; the names may change but the symptoms and struggles do not. Those who have been threatened with death, sexual violence, or other serious harm may develop PTSD, as may those who experience the death of a close family member or friend. Indirect rather than direct exposure is possible for causation as well, such as a police officer who has seen the aftermath of terrible things like child abuse. These types of traumatic/threatening incidents must be experienced before a person will typically be diagnosed with PTSD.

The seven most common root causes of PTSD are as follows:

1. Combat and various forms of military training
2. Assaults, sexual or physical
3. Learning about a loved one's violent or accidental death or injury
4. Sexual or physical abuse of children
5. Serious mishaps
6. Natural disasters, wildfires, and so forth.
7. Terrorist attacks

PTSD affects people of all backgrounds, regardless of race, nationality, or culture. In fact, one in every eleven people will be diagnosed with the disorder at some point in their lives, and 3.5% of American adults will experience its symptoms on a yearly basis, according to current estimates. More women than men suffer from PTSD, and the disorder is more common in people in the US who are Latino, African American, or American Indian. There is evidence to suggest that African Americans, Latino Americans, and American Indians experience higher rates of PTSD in the US due to a variety of factors, including exposure to violence and discrimination. However, it is important to note that research on this topic is ongoing and that individual experiences may vary.

Those who suffer from PTSD can have troubling thoughts and feelings persist long after the traumatic incident occurred. They may have dreams or flashbacks and may experience sadness, fear, or rage, as well as a sense of separation or alienation from others. If you're among those suffering from PTSD, try to stay away from people or places that remind you of the trauma. For example, that may mean avoiding being near loud noises or in situations where people may invade your space and be apt to touch you.

SYMPTOMS OF PTSD

PTSD symptoms can be broken down into the following four groups, with the severity of specific symptoms varying.

1. **Memories are repeated involuntarily:** This may include intrusive thoughts related to the trauma, such as disturbing nightmares or flashbacks. If the horrific event is so vivid that it feels like it's happening right in front of your eyes, you may be having a flashback.
2. **Avoidance:** With this common symptom, you stay away from people, places, activities, items, and events that may cause upsetting memories, in an effort to forget or avoid reliving the traumatic incident. You may also be reluctant to talk about and share what transpired or how you feel about it.
3. **Negative thoughts/unhappiness:** "I am horrible," "No one can be trusted," and other negative thoughts and sentiments may arise as false beliefs that you have about yourself or others. You may also have trouble finding even small bits of happiness or satisfaction, as well as feelings of distance or estrangement.
4. **Hypervigilance and arousal:** You may find yourself in a changed state of hypervigilance and responsiveness, which

can make you angry and irritable; act recklessly or in a self-destructive way; be suspicious of your surroundings; or have a hard time concentrating or getting enough sleep.

While those symptoms point to PTSD, there are different subtypes of stress response that may—or may not—lead to PTSD developing.

PTSD IS CLASSIFIED INTO THREE TYPES WITH TWO PRECEDING STRESS RESPONSES/DISORDERS

Normal Stress Response: A person's normal stress response can be triggered by a variety of events, including but not limited to accidents, illnesses, operations, and other situations involving an excessive level of tension or stress. If you're having a hard time handling stress, you may benefit from counseling. People who have normal stress responses should start to feel better in a few weeks.

Acute Stress Disorder: When a person experiences a life-threatening event, they may develop an acute stress disorder, which is not the same as PTSD. An acute stress disorder is typically short term and generally situational. Some situational stress, however, can become long-term. Acute stress disorder can be triggered by natural disasters, the loss of loved ones, the loss of a job, or the fear of death. Without treatment, acute stress disorder could progress to PTSD. Those who have acute stress disorder may benefit from individual or group therapy, medications, and a treatment regimen from a psychiatrist.

1. **Uncomplicated PTSD:** The most uncomplicated form of PTSD to treat is simple PTSD, which can be traced back to a single, big traumatic event. Trauma avoidance, night

terrors, flashbacks, irritability, mood swings, and changes in interpersonal interactions are all signs of simple PTSD. Therapy, medication, or a combination of the two can be used to treat mild symptoms of simple, uncomplicated PTSD.

2. **Complex PTSD:** Complex PTSD, or C-PTSD, is a far more severe form of PTSD. Multiple traumas, not just one, are to blame. Abuse or interpersonal violence, repeated exposure to war or communal violence, or abrupt bereavement can all lead to complex PTSD. Treatment for complex PTSD is more intensive than for uncomplicated PTSD, even though some symptoms may be similar. The more complex form, however, may include borderline or antisocial personality disorder, dissociative disorders, and behaviors such as impetuosity and violence. If you have underlying bipolar disorder, which has been known to include both anxiety and depression at the same time, it can add even further to the stress levels with complex PTSD.

3. **Comorbid PTSD:** Comorbid PTSD is the term used to describe those who have both PTSD and another mental illness—co-occurring conditions. This may encompass a wide range of mental health issues, often accompanied by drug abuse issues. Many have co-occurring PTSD, and it is not uncommon for a person to try to treat the illness without the help of a mental health professional. In some cases, this can include self-medication and other harmful activities. The use of drugs or alcohol to make the pain go away will only make things worse—along with making treatment more time consuming. If you fall into this category, you may definitely benefit from treating both the co-occurring mental health problems and PTSD in tandem for the most effective results.

PTSD HAS SEVEN ROOT CAUSES

If you or someone you know experiences a life-threatening event, you may suffer from PTSD. PTSD can be caused by a variety of things, the most common of which are listed below:

1. Combat and various forms of military training
2. Assaults, sexual or physical
3. Learning about a loved one's violent or accidental death or injury
4. Sexual or physical abuse of children
5. Serious mishaps
6. Natural disasters, wildfires, and so forth.
7. Terrorist attacks

GETTING HELP

A DIAGNOSIS OF PTSD

TO BE DIAGNOSED WITH PTSD, you must have experienced one or more traumatic events, as defined by the Diagnostic and Statistical Manual of Mental Disorders, Fifth Edition (DSM-5), which means being exposed to the danger of death or serious injury including sexual assault. It is not required to have direct experience of the event. Indirect exposure may also be contributors, such as:

- Witnessing someone else's traumatic event
- Hearing about a close friend or relative's violent or accidental death, the meaning of which might be hard for you to comprehend
- Being privy to disturbing details, such as a police officer hearing details about repeated child sexual abuse

PTSD symptoms are investigated for a diagnosis after exposure has occurred. According to DSM-5, for a diagnosis of PTSD you must meet the following conditions:

- The traumatizing experience is relived
- Symptoms include an incursion of traumatic memories or thoughts
- Avoidance symptoms include (but are not limited to)
  - Avoidance of thoughts and feelings
  - Avoidance of activity
  - Avoidance of memory
- Two or more signs indicate a deterioration in mood and feelings
- Two or more signs of arousal or reactivity change

In addition to these signs and symptoms

- Condition lasts for at least a month.
- Your life must be severely disrupted and/or affected in a significant way.
- Medical conditions or substance abuse are not acceptable explanations

The DSM has undergone a number of changes over time regarding trauma and stressor-related disorders. In DSM-5, PTSD is no longer classified as an anxiety disorder as it was in the past but instead as a "Trauma and Stressor Related Disorder."

Among the most significant alterations in DSM-5 compared to the earlier DSM-IV edition are the following:

- Traumatic incidents are defined more clearly
- Traumatic exposure is expanded beyond those who experienced or witnessed it to include others close to the situation and/or exposed to details (not through media)
- The number of symptom groups grew, with avoidance symptoms broken into its own grouping
- Wording for some symptoms was rephrased in a more accurate manner
- New criteria for children under the age of six was added
- Acute and chronic stages were eliminated
- Dissociative features became a brand-new specifier

PTSD TREATMENTS

There are many ways for doctors to help you as a PTSD patient. In the early stages of the intervention clinicians— Licensed Clinical Social Workers, licensed counselors, nurses, dieticians, pharmacists, activity therapists, or other professionals that are part of the patients' treatment team—should ask for help or supervision from those with experience. Below are frequently relied upon PTSD treatments:

1. **Cognitive Behavioral Therapy (CBT).** CBT is used by clinical psychologists to help you understand how your thoughts, feelings, and behaviors all work together, as well as understanding the root causes of your problems.

2. **Cognitive Processing Therapy (CPT).** This is a specific form of cognitive-behavioral therapy that teaches you how to identify, confront, and deal with harmful beliefs that you have about your trauma.
3. **Cognitive Therapy.** This type of therapy, based on cognitive behavioral therapy, tries to change your negative evaluations and memories of trauma and is used to help you if you have trouble with behavior or mental health.
4. **Prolonged Exposure (PET).** This cognitive-behavioral therapy is aimed at guiding you through the traumatic events that occurred to help you process the memories and feelings, thereby breaking your association of certain everyday cues that you might link to trauma-related memories.
5. **Brief Eclectic Psychotherapy.** Cognitive Behavioral Therapy and psychodynamic approaches are combined in a brief eclectic psychotherapy session. Shame and guilt, as well as the relationship between the therapist and you as the patient, are discussed.
6. **Eye Movement Desensitization and Reprocessing (EMDR) Therapy.** This involves bilateral stimulation (usually eye movements) while you focus on the trauma memory for a short time. EMDR is aimed at helping your trauma memories become less clear and intense.
7. **Narrative Exposure Therapy (NET).** Narrative exposure therapy aids in the development of a life narrative in which traumatic experiences can be understood. It is well-known for its application in refugee group therapy.

Learn more at: https://www.apa.org/ptsd-guideline/treatments

In addition to the psychotherapies noted above, there are also neurological therapies, medications, and self-help tools. Let's delve into these options more.

WHAT ARE THE TREATMENT OPTIONS FOR PTSD?

- Psychotherapy
- Neurological therapies
- Medications
- Self-help/at-home coping tools

In the event of a traumatic incident, the body releases a surge of hormones to make you ready to fight, flee, or freeze. You may experience a narrowing of your field of vision, a loss of short-term memory, and a feeling of fear. Trauma can have a profound influence on the body, mind, and spirit. People who have PTSD have symptoms that can last a long time or get in the way of their daily lives. Those with PTSD can benefit from a variety of therapy approaches and medications, and many studies have been conducted to determine those most effective. Let's take a closer look at options:

ADVANTAGES OF THERAPY

Certain types of therapy may provide potential benefits in the treatment of PTSD symptoms. including:

- Alleviating anxiety
- Symptomatic relief from depression
- Lowering the chances of a recurrence of depressive symptoms

- Enhancing abilities that are required for daily tasks: problem-solving enhancement; insight building; options building; recognition of patterns

Psychotherapy

There are successful treatments for PTSD in psychotherapy, often known as talk therapy. If you're having problems with your thoughts, cognitive behavioral therapy (CBT) can help you figure out what you're thinking and how to change it.

Cognitive processing therapy

Cognitive Processing Therapy (CPT) is based on the belief that you may not have been able to fully comprehend what happened to you immediately following a trauma. An investigation into what happened can lead to judgments that are not healthy in the long run. It's possible that you'll come to believe that no one can be trusted or that you're at fault for what happened. The goal of CPT is to detect and reframe any erroneous judgments. There are about twelve sessions in this sort of treatment where you and your therapist talk or write about what transpired over the course of that time period.

Prolonged exposure therapy

Prolonged exposure treatment, like CPT, aims to combat the tendency to develop problematic thought habits following a traumatic incident. For example, you may have developed an excessive fear reaction because of your trauma. Prolonged exposure therapy begins by teaching you about the symptoms of PTSD to help you overcome your fear. When you face a stressful situation, your therapist will teach you how to calm down and cope. You and your therapist will develop a fear hierarchy after you've learned self-calming skills. Matching triggers that activate with calming coping strategies. You'll begin with mildly unnerving anxieties and work your way up to more acute ones, some of which may be connected to the trauma you've been through. You and your therapist must both be satisfied that you can manage each stage before you can move on to the next. Your therapist will help you deal with your fears and worries while also teaching you new ways to deal with them. With the help of your therapist, you'll learn that your traumatic thoughts and memories aren't dangerous or unpleasant.

Neurological Therapies

In the long term, PTSD can have a significant impact on your brain health. Thus, treatments that focus on the brain and neurological system are very good at getting people back to work and easing their symptoms.

Eye Movement Desensitization and Reprocessing (EMDR)

As part of the EMDR process, you'll use repetitive eye movements to break up and reset memories associated with trauma. Learning how to deal with memories and the emotions they generate will lead to a more optimistic outlook on life. The World Health Organization (WHO) recommends this treatment for PTSD since it is low-cost and has few side effects, if any at all.

Emotional Freedom Technique (EFT or Tapping)

A technique known as the Therapeutic Emotional Liberation Technique incorporates tapping as a component, known as emotional freedom technique (EFT). It's similar to acupressure, which is a massage technique that relies on applying pressure to certain parts of the skin in order to relieve symptoms like pain and muscle stiffness. In the case of EFT, it involves touching certain points on your body where the flow of energy gets blocked—primarily on the head and face—while actively imagining an event that was painful. Cognitive and exposure therapies frequently incorporate tapping into their treatment plans, and some PTSD symptoms such as anxiety, despair, and physical discomfort may be eased by EFT therapy. The stress hormone cortisol may also be reduced by EFT treatments. With the help of an expert, you can learn how to do EFT yourself, typically in four to ten sessions, but it's important to learn the technique with a qualified therapist first, even if you plan to use it on your own later.

Medication

The American Psychological Association (APA) recommends antidepressants for the treatment of PTSD. These are selective serotonin re-uptake inhibitors (SSRIs) including:

- Fluoxetine (Prozac)
- Sertraline (Zoloft)
- Paroxetine (Paxil) *If started on Paxil, make sure the dry dose is not missed!

To date, the FDA has only approved the use of paroxetine and sertraline as treatments for PTSD.

For some complex PTSD, other drugs used and found to be effective are mood-stabilizers such as: Carbamazepine, valproate, topiramate, lamotrigine, lithium, and gabapentin.

SELF-HELP/AT-HOME COPING: WHAT CAN YOU DO TO IMPROVE YOUR OWN SITUATION?

The quick answer is a lot. Recognizing the talents that helped you survive the trauma is a smart place to start, even if those skills aren't particularly useful to you right now. People who have been through a lot of trauma can use many different tools to help them get over their PTSD symptoms and get back to feeling good about themselves.

Write

PTSD symptoms may be alleviated by journaling over time about the distressing incident. There can also be relief just by writing about things that have happened in your life that have been hard for you. Numerous studies have shown writing therapy can help you get better faster.

Try yoga or meditation

Patients with PTSD can benefit from complementary therapies such as meditation and yoga, or any safe relaxation technique that works for that individual. In addition to therapy and medicine, these activities can help you regulate your breathing and become more conscious of your own body.

Explore online therapy options

Online counseling gives you flexibility to participate in treatment sessions from the convenience of your own home or office—whether via your phone, computer, or an app. Such sessions may also be less intimidating and more accessible than other forms of treatments you need.

THE NATIONAL CENTER FOR PTSD PROVIDES A WIDE RANGE OF RESOURCES

- Apps such as PTSD Coach, Insomnia Coach, and Mindfulness Coach
- Comprehensive video tutorials on symptoms and treatment

- https://www.ptsd.va.gov/appvid/decisionaid_public.asp This site can help you determine the best course of action in your situation.
- Stress, anger, parenting concerns, and sleep issues can all be addressed through online classes.

WHAT TO LOOK FOR IN A THERAPIST AND HOW TO CHOOSE THE APPROPRIATE ONE

Consider the following choices when searching for a therapist who can help you with PTSD:

- Look for a therapist who has received specific training in the PTSD field to help you recover from your trauma
- To keep expenses down, consult the provider network within your insurance program
- The search engine of the Association for Behavioral and Cognitive Therapies is also a great place for locating clinicians
- Seek referrals from someone you trust such as friends, coworkers, or organizations that specialize in trauma recovery
- Make a list of the qualities in a therapist that would make you feel comfortable and understood. Do you wish to work with a therapist who is openly LGBTQ+? Someone with whom you have similar religious, racial, or gender identities?
- Think about the distance. Is the therapist close to where you live or work? Do they have virtual appointments?
- Make sure the therapist licensed in your state
- Finally, allow yourself the freedom to switch therapists when needs change or the fit is not right.

It is possible that your initial choice of a therapist will not be the right one for you. Think of your first session as an interview; you're not bound if the fit's not right.

INSURANCE AND COSTS

Although deductibles and copayments vary from policy to policy, most insurance policies cover some mental health services. All three versions of Medicare, as well as Medicare Advantage and Medicaid, cover mental health services to some degree. To find affordable PTSD therapy without health insurance, look for a therapist who charges on a sliding scale. This search engine could be helpful (https://www.goodtherapy.org/). Another potential choice is the Open Path Psychotherapy Collective. And if you're looking for low-cost or no-cost therapy, a local community mental health clinic is a great place to start.

A look at some of the alternatives to trauma-focused therapy is next on our list of things to think about!

NON-TRAUMA-FOCUSED THERAPIES

There's a wide range of non-trauma-based therapies that can provide comfort, relief, and healing from PTSD. It's not one-size-fits all but, rather, finding the techniques that are of most interest to you personally—and most rewarding in their results. These range from conditioning your neural pathways to better appreciating your good behaviors, to anxiety management tools, talk therapy, journaling, aromatherapy, equine-assisted therapy,

NEURO-ASSOCIATIVE CONDITIONING

Break bad habits for good.

There is a "pleasure circuit" in the human brain. This pleasure circuit, which is more highly evolved in humans than in other species, is a remarkable feature. For example, if we help others, exercise, and meditate, our pleasure circuit will reward us. Short-term remedies like sweet foods, alcohol, and narcotics are what the pleasure circuit craves when it is at its worst. The human brain is flexible. A serious injury to it can be repaired. It is capable of mastering a wide range of new abilities. Our brain and its pleasure circuits can be reprogrammed in whatever way we choose, thanks to the term "plasticity." Neuro-associative conditioning can assist us in this endeavor. But what precisely is neuro-associative conditioning? How can you put it to use to attain your goals?

Neural association involves neural pathways that link the human experience with a series of associations, such as pleasure or pain, and those associations are involved in motivating behavior. Neuro-associative conditioning involves creating a new framework of behaviors and associations. Elements of this concept go as far back as Aristotle and Plato. The concept, however, has been popularized in current times by Tony Robbins. Using neuro-associative conditioning, you can change your life for the better, establishing new pathways to transform your thinking and your life for the better. Here are steps to condition new behaviors:

Step one: Decide

The first step toward achieving any goal is deciding what you want to strive toward from a positive perspective. There are far too many individuals who spend their lives focusing on the things they don't want and if you're among them, you may remain alone and unwell or locked into an unfulfilling career. In the first phase of neuro-associative conditioning, you need to dive deeper and ask yourself, "What do I really want?" As much as possible, be specific, such as "Weight loss and running a mile in ten minutes are my goals." Or, "You know, I'm thinking of starting up my own software development firm soon." Neuro-associative conditioning relies on a solid foundation, and the first step is to lay that foundation by getting laser-focused on your goals.

Step two: Leverage

Brain reprogramming is required to completely commit to the task. When you use neuro-associative programming, you'll link huge joy with attaining your goals and massive suffering with any behaviors that detract from them. Qualifying self-inquiries like, "How much would it cost me if I didn't make this change?" can help. "Upon achieving my goals, what will I feel like?" In your old age, imagine yourself reminiscing about your past. Make a mental picture of the answers to both those questions. If you've never left your job to start your own business that you've dreamed of, your life may be riddled with regret and boredom. Or, you could have taken a chance and ended up living a life full of adventure, excitement, and success. Is there any room for compromise? Necessary steps or requirements to attain your goals may need modifications/adjustments along the way.

Step three: Interrupt

Using neuro-associative conditioning, you will not settle for anything less than attaining your objectives—avoiding any obstacles to achieving your goals. What are your limiting beliefs, and how are they keeping you from achieving your full potential? Despite the fact that they don't serve us, we're all plagued by negative thoughts and actions that stem from our upbringing and previous experiences. To feel better, that may mean you grab that second piece of cake that you don't really need. You can break this pattern if you realize it. A hard slap on the back of your own hand is all that is needed. Put the television in the closet when you're tempted to watch Netflix instead of working on your business plan. When you have neuro-associative conditioning, you will be taught to link your bad habits with bad results instead of good ones.

Step four: Create

Neuro-associative training involves more than just tying pain to bad behavior. Those outmoded habits must be swapped out for more positive ones if you want to see a change. You want to create a structure for goal attainment. Eat a healthy snack and pretend it's as good as that slice of cake. Instead of going to the fridge, go for a walk after you stand up. Journaling, meditation, or visualization practices can help you achieve your goals instead of watching Netflix. The use of models is also a useful method here: Be inspired by the life you wish to lead by studying someone who has already achieved the type of life you aspire to. By following their lead, you can build a route to success like theirs.

Step five: Condition

The reward area of your brain is rebuilt by neuro-associative conditioning. The more you practice your new habits, the more your brain sends out "reward chemicals" like serotonin and dopamine. Productivity leads to positivity! New habits can lead to experiences that are even more rewarding than those associated with old ones because of the molecules' role in creating a new neural pathway. It becomes more fulfilling to consume a nutritious diet than to receive a sugar rush from a piece of cake. When you add a morning ritual into your daily routine, you feel more focused and motivated throughout the day. The only thing you need to do is keep up with your positive behaviors. Your brain will do the rest if you give it the correct neuro-associative programming.

Step six: Test

All new habits are put to the test eventually. On vacation, for example, you may be lured by an unending spread of food. The next day, you'll have trouble concentrating and will be groggy from the effects of going out late the night before. A visualization approach known as "future pacing" can help you avoid temptation by measuring the intensity of your neuro-associative conditioning. Imagine yourself in a situation, such as at a buffet or receiving a text message inviting you to happy hour. What choices do you have? What are the repercussions of your actions? What exactly do you do for a living? Retrace your steps to step five if you make a mistake and keep practicing until you've mastered the new behavior. Throughout these steps maintain balance.

PTSD ANXIETY MANAGEMENT TECHNIQUES THAT ARE EFFECTIVE:

If you have PTSD, chances are you are generally plagued by frequent and acute anxiety symptoms. It may be common for you to turn to inappropriate methods of coping to deal with your anxieties. Fortunately, anxiety may be managed well in many ways. Anxiety can be reduced in severity, frequency, and/or tolerability by employing these following anxiety management methods:

Deep Breathing

It may sound odd, but many people forget to breathe correctly. Your diaphragm, a huge muscle in your abdomen, is involved in natural breathing. When you inhale, you should feel your tummy rise. Your tummy should drop when you exhale. As you get older, however, you lose the ability to breathe using the diaphragm and instead may rely more on the chest and shoulders. Inhaling too quickly might lead to a rise in stress and anxiety. But fortunately, you can retrain your diaphragm to breathe deeply again so that you can better cope with stress. Deep breathing exercises can help alleviate stress and anxiety.

Progressive Muscle Relaxation

Stress and anxiety can be effectively reduced by the practice of relaxation exercises. Your muscles relax when you tighten and release different sections of your body. This method of relaxation resembles a pendulum in its action. You must first tense your muscles to achieve total relaxation. You might feel your muscles tighten when you're stressed, which can be a signal to calm down if you do so often. When that happens, try to relax your muscles right away. Combine deep breathing with progressive muscle relaxation for a fuller and even better effect.

Mindfulness

Anxiety sufferers may find great relief with the application of mindfulness techniques. Mindfulness has existed for a long time— a state of being in the here and now—and mental health practitioners are beginning to realize that mindfulness might have benefits for those battling anxiety or sadness. We spend a lot of time in our brains worrying about the stresses of daily life. When you start practicing mindfulness, it can help you get your mind off things and pay attention to what is going on right now—present sensory awareness and feeling gratitude in the moment.

Self-Monitoring

As a means of coping with anxiety, self-monitoring is a good idea. We all tend to stick to routines. It is common for us to go about our daily routines without giving much thought to what is going on around us. A lack of awareness can be helpful in some instances, but it can also leave us with the impression that our thoughts and emotions are uncontrollable and unpredictable. Anxiety symptoms can't be effectively addressed until we know what triggers these feelings. Simple self-monitoring is a great way to become aware of your own conduct.

Social Support

Not surprisingly, numerous studies show that those who have experienced a terrible event and PTSD can benefit greatly from receiving support from others. Having someone you can confide in when you're going through a tough time or need some emotional support is a lifesaver. Just knowing you have a listening ear is helpful, but it may not be sufficient in and of itself. A professional-led support group may be a good option if you are struggling with anxiety because such a group can provide many components of a supportive relationship.

Self-Soothing

The ability to cope with anxiety is essential when you're experiencing it. Spending time with other people can be extremely beneficial to your emotional and physical well-being. Anxiety-related symptoms of PTSD, however, might strike without warning and without the benefit of nearby social support. As a result, it is imperative that you acquire self-help coping mechanisms. These self-soothing or self-care strategies are meant to help you feel better and less stressed, such as: aroma therapy, a hot bath, giving yourself a butterfly hug, or self-massage of your neck, arms, legs, hands, or feet. Consider sitting or walking along the beach or by a body of water. Take a walk amid nature, in the countryside, or stroll a city. Look at pictures of loved ones. Eat a good meal or desert. Spend time with a loved one and enjoy intimacy. Or pursue any other healthy, soothing event that appeals to any of your five senses that you find relaxing.

Expressive Writing

Journaling, also known as expressive writing, can help your anxiety by allowing you to process and express your ideas and feelings. It has been well-researched that expressive writing has a lot of benefits for both your body and your mind. People who have PTSD, who write about how they feel, have been found to be better able to deal with things, make good changes to their lives after a bad thing happens, and lessen their PTSD symptoms, anxiety, and rage.

Distraction

To cope with powerful and painful emotions like worry and dread, deliberate use of distraction methods might be beneficial. Anything you do to briefly divert your focus away from an intense feeling is considered a form of distraction. Focusing on a strong emotion can amplify its intensity and sense of powerlessness. As a result, you may be able to lessen the intensity of the emotion by taking a break from it for a short period of time.

Behavioral Activation

There is a strong correlation between anxiety and the desire to avoid stressful situations. However, in the long run, avoiding anxiety-inducing situations may lead to a less fulfilling and meaningful existence, especially if this avoidance grows larger and larger in its impact. Increasing your level of activity and the amount of time you spend on enjoyable and fulfilling activities is possible through a process known as behavioral activation. Behavioral activation focuses on changing behaviors to address problems you might be experiencing. Originally developed to treat depression, its goal is to increase activity levels (and prevent avoidance behaviors) and help you take part in positive and rewarding activities that can improve mood. Through behavioral activation, depression and anxiety symptoms can be alleviated.

HOW PTSD IS TREATED BY STRESS INOCULATION TRAINING

PTSD is a condition that can be treated with stress inoculation training, or SIT for short, a form of cognitive-behavioral therapy. This type of therapy, a form of talk therapy, can help you identify and modify the inaccurate and/or negative beliefs that are driving your behavior. Stress inoculation training is a common form of psychotherapy.

Stress Inoculation Training (SIT)

People with PTSD often have anxiety and nightmares. Stress inoculation training is like getting a vaccine that can help protect you from these symptoms, but in this case the vaccine is like an anti-triggering vaccine. With stress inoculation training, you are exposed to manageable levels of stress and anxiety that allow you to build up your self-esteem and improve your ability to deal with stressful situations more quickly and effectively. This may involve numerous 90-minute sessions, spread out over a period of time, and it's typically done with a therapist one-on-one rather than in a group.

Stress Inoculation Training (SIT) Techniques

You develop the ability to cope. If you suffer from PTSD, your therapist can help you learn how to recognize and avoid the triggers that set off your worry and panic. You'll also learn about a variety of anxiety-relieving techniques, such as:

- **Deep diaphragmatic breathing**: Take two deep breaths in and two deep breaths out. The first step in this coping training is to learn how to breathe deeply. Then, outside of treatment, you should keep practicing so that it becomes a healthy habit.
- **Develop the ability to talk to oneself**: Even if you already do this on a regular basis, as many people with and without PTSD do, stress inoculation training instructs you to sharpen your internal monologue so that you can more quickly identify and stop negative statements about yourself in favor of encouraging ones.
- **Exercises for muscle relaxation**: By tensing and releasing each of your major muscle groups in the correct manner, you'll learn how to relax them. Recorded versions of these exercises can be used at home between therapist training sessions.
- **Role-playing:** This is when you begin to put the coping skills you've learned into practice. You and your therapist make up a situation that makes you anxious, and then together you practice dealing with it.
- **Contemplating and modifying negative behaviors**: This involves practicing successful coping by using your imagination. Your therapist will guide you through a stressful situation so that you can learn to recognize the signs of trauma and take the right steps to minimize the impact.

With SIT, you also learn how to put what you've learned into practice. You and your therapist will work together to learn how to recognize the signs that can set off your worry and panic and how to deal with them as soon as they occur. This way, you can immediately use the coping skills you've learned to deal with your worries and stress before they get out of hand.

These SIT techniques are all good tools! The problem is when you are taught the tools but don't practice them—and forget them. I recommend maintaining a list and regularly practicing techniques so if freezing occurs, you can refer to the list for help.

USING ESSENTIAL OILS TO TREAT PTSD: A QUICK GUIDE

Aromatherapy can help alleviate the symptoms of PTSD. And, while aromatherapy is safe when used appropriately, essential oils can be potent, so you need to be aware of their potential dangers. Aromatherapy should be individualized with your provider's input, given personal sensitivities. They should not be used on the skin directly unless mixed with another oil such as sunflower. In order to avoid potentially harmful interactions with drugs or other health issues, it is best to use high-quality, pure oils wherever possible and understand each oil's contraindications carefully before using. Pregnant women should avoid using oils that are known to harm the unborn children. Before using essential oils on your own, ask an aromatherapist for help if you're not sure.

Therapeutic Essential Oils for Post-Traumatic Stress Disorder:

Lavender essential oil can help alleviate fear, anxiety, tension, panic, and despair, as well as minimize nightmares and sleep disruptions, making it an excellent essential oil for PTSD. You may also find that ylang-ylang and clary sage might help alleviate your feelings of anxiety and panic. For people who have PTSD, the smell of frankincense, chamomile, and sandalwood can help.

You could try helichrysum serotinum, one of the most vital essential oils if you are suffering from PTSD. Helichrysum serotinum provides the same healing properties as helichrysum italicum, but it is also noted for its ability to reach and resolve deep-seated emotional difficulties. Because of its calming aroma, you may be able to get in touch with sentiments and emotions that have been suppressed for a long time. It's a useful technique for processing and emotional healing of injuries like PTSD since it can help retrieve forgotten memories. Diluting it to 2% in any carrier oil (ten drops per tablespoon) and applying it to the areas where you feel discomfort may be a good option for you (e.g. the temples, the chest/heart area, etc.). Because of its potency, only if you're familiar with the scent should you use helichrysum serotinum on yourself or a loved one for the purpose of enhancing emotional well-being.

People respond differently to various essential oils just as different treatments work well on different people. Rose can help some people deal with grief. Massage the heart area with diluted organic rose otto essential oil, the most soothing sort of rose oil. In most cases, you'll want to dilute it to 2% in any carrier oil (10 drops per tablespoon). You might also add a few drops to a bath to relax.

Cistus (sometimes known as "rockrose," even though it isn't connected to the rose family) is another essential oil widely used for trauma. A diffuser can be used to spread the oil around. It can also be used in massages (diluted to 2% in a carrier oil with ten drops per tablespoon) or soothing baths (diluted to 2% in a carrier oil with 10 drops per tablespoon). Depending on your symptoms, Anxiety-Free Roll-On Relief or Anxiety-Free Synergy may potentially be helpful. For some, Stress-Free Roll-On Relief or Stress-Free Synergy is more appealing. You can also try Deep Rest Synergy or Deep Rest Roll-On Relief if you're having problems falling asleep.

Essential oils can be used topically by diluting them and applying them sparingly to the skin. A moisturizing lotion with a few drops of essential oil could be used each day to keep your hands and arms soft and moist. Many people use essential oils in their baths. Oils' therapeutic scent can be released by a few drops in the water, and the act of having a relaxing bath can also help alleviate feelings of stress or worry. You can also add a few drops of essential oil to the water chamber of your diffuser and let it circulate throughout your home and/or spray pillows, drapes, cushions, sofas, and other soft furniture with a mixture of essential oils and water.

HEALING PTSD WITH EQUINE THERAPY

Equine-assisted therapy for veterans with PTSD is currently being investigated at Columbia University Irving Medical Center by Yuval Neria, PhD., and Prudence Fisher, PhD. Both are also directors of the Trauma and PTSD Program and researchers at the New York State Psychiatric Institute. They co-founded the Man O' War Project, which develops and tests the efficacy of equine-assisted therapy for vets who have PTSD. This was the first university-led research study to lay out specific recommendations for how to use it. Earle I. Mack, a veteran, and thoroughbred owner and breeder came up with the idea for the project. He gave his time and money to make it happen. In Mack's view, horses could have a positive impact on human psychopathology.

Veterans are said to suffer from PTSD at a rate of 30%. Dr. Fisher notes the wide spectrum of symptoms ranging from flashbacks and nightmares to rage, negative thoughts, severe anxiety, and hypervigilance, as well as substance misuse and the risk of suicide. The Department of Veterans Affairs estimates that at least twenty-two veterans take their own lives every day. Current treatments like cognitive behavioral therapy and exposure therapy, meanwhile, have high dropout rates and are ineffective. As Dr. Neria points out, even the most successful treatments and medications for PTSD only help half of the general PTSD population, and that number drops much lower among veterans. Dr. Jeffrey A. Lieberman of New York-Presbyterian/Columbia Hospital says, "It's doubly terrible since this problem should be solved—from the standpoint of how scientifically demanding or tough it may be to grasp."

The Man of War Initiative

Matthew Ryba, a US Marine sergeant, feels that equine therapy can help veterans who are suffering from PTSD. Says Dr. Fisher, "Horses and individuals with PTSD are both hypervigilant because of their temperament." Getting to the root of this problem was the main goal of the therapy plan, which included a series of structured exercises at an equestrian center over eight weeks, that helped the two participants work through their ongoing trauma-related functioning issues.

"Veterans can get useful feedback about their communication styles from horses," adds Dr. Neria. This allows veterans to learn from their mistakes, and horses are gentle and nonjudgmental. According to the experts, connections with horses must be earned, in contrast to those with dogs, which give love without conditions. This earning of trust is important for veterans with PTSD, who must learn how to build trust in themselves and others again so that they can be successful in their families, workplaces, and social circles.

Pre-and post-MRIs were conducted in the research to see if there were any brain alterations as a result of therapy. The findings revealed that equine-assisted therapy created structural and functional changes in the brain in areas associated with reward-seeking and pleasure. The therapy was shown to be incredibly promising: it was completed by 92% of participants, found to be beneficial to men and women across age groups and military history, and resulted in significant improvement in PTSD and depression symptoms.

According to Dr. Lieberman, "Horses produce a safe relational engagement, more so than any creature or even any person. This causes a temporary reduction in the individual's hypervigilance and unpleasant emotionality connected with the traumatizing experience." As the therapy is given over and over again, the unpleasant, intense emotional part of the patient's traumatic experience lessens.

Author's note: I've personally found equine-assisted therapy to be the most effective non-trauma focused therapy. However, I did have other therapies in my toolbox prior to attending equine-assisted therapy at a HOOVES (Healing Of Our Veterans through Equine Services) retreat.

INNOVATIVE TREATMENTS FOR PTSD

PTSD can be treated with a variety of other methods. Some additional innovations in the field include those below.

Virtual Reality Exposure

Virtual reality exposure therapy (VRET) allows you to gradually be exposed to your traumatic circumstances while working closely with a skilled clinician, allowing you to overcome the trauma. When you go through exposure therapy, you can face parts of your trauma with less fear and try to get used to the way it makes you feel. This can help with a wide range of anxiety disorders. You and the clinician work together to keep you from having the traumatic experience by manipulating visual conditions and talking about them in a safe environment. As one veteran put it, "It's as if you're going through the story a million times in your head. In the end, my story failed to inspire an emotional response because I had grown tired of telling it."

Ketamine Infusion

Ketamine infusions, which were first approved by the FDA to be used as an anesthetic, can be used to treat mental health problems like PTSD. Low doses of ketamine are delivered intravenously, making it safe for in-office use without creating significant side effects. A single forty-minute infusion treatment has been shown to have a big impact on the symptoms of PTSD. There is a wide range of illnesses that can be treated with a course of ketamine injections, but only medical experts who have been trained and approved to deliver infusions can give them. Current research has been looking into the best delivery methods over longer periods of time.

MDMA-Assisted Therapy

Ecstasy is a popular recreational drug that contains MDMA, a synthetic drug that alters mood and perception. Researchers are looking into the use of MDMA in the treatment of mental health issues such as PTSD. In MDMA-assisted therapy, the impact of a traumatic experience is said to be less threatening when you process it with your therapist while under the influence of the drug. MDMA-assisted treatment is non-directive, i.e. the therapist refrains from interpretation or explanation but encourages you to talk freely without judgement, so you don't have to worry about being judged or pressured by others. It is claimed that MDMA can help you access your traumatic memories without fear of threat, making it easier for you to process your thoughts and feelings about the experience. This alternative treatment is still being investigated to see if it has any risks. This therapy is considered quite controversial by some therapists.

As you can see from the above therapies for PTSD, there is a gamut of possibilities. One other possible service of note is obtaining a service and support dog, which many find to be very helpful.

If you are part of a family, however, it is imperative that you involve them in your recovery. In the next chapter, you'll learn how to incorporate your entire family into your recovery process.

THE FAMILY'S ROLE

REDUCING THE IMPACT OF PTSD ON A LOVED ONE

PTSD IS A PARTICULARLY difficult issue for families to deal with once a soldier returns from a combat zone. Veterans with PTSD and their families face additional challenges throughout the transition from military service to civilian life. Families understandably want to know what they can do to assist their loved ones who have PTSD. Let us hope that these suggestions will help you begin the journey of recovery.

Learn everything you can About PTSD

A detailed understanding of PTSD is necessary before family members can help a PTSD sufferer. Reading books, performing internet research, and talking to other families who have been through PTSD can give you a clearer picture of the struggles your loved one is facing. Children should be able to ask their parents about PTSD and receive an age-appropriate explanation.

Anticipate PTSD triggers

It's upsetting to witness someone you care about struggling with symptoms when a life event triggers them. First, you may not know what your loved one's emotional triggers are, and you may not know how their reaction would make you feel. It's possible that your loved one doesn't even realize they have triggers until they experience them, which makes it even more difficult. PTSD triggers are described below, even though they may be different for each person.

Common PTSD triggers:

- Listening to news reports about similar incidents to the trauma experienced
- Significant milestones, such as the anniversary date of the trauma's occurrence
- Remembering the experience by reliving it in the environment through the senses whether a smell, sound, an object seen, rubbing up against something ... even a taste can trigger a memory.
- Attending medical appointments, attending funerals, or being hospitalized

Identifying triggers for your family member's PTSD will make it easier for you to stay away from those circumstances in the future.

Allow yourself to be receptive to what others have to say

It is important for family members of veterans with PTSD to listen to them without disruption or judgment. By doing so, you increase your loved one's likelihood of opening up and discussing their distressing experience. Anxiety is a common symptom of PTSD. Your loved one may need more assurances that you're there to help them and that they have no power to drive you away.

Make no demands on your loved one's time to process their PTSD

Everyone's reaction to PTSD is unique. Some people are ready to talk about their trauma straight away, while others may take months or even years before they are even able to begin the process of reliving their experience. A family member's desire to see their loved one recover might be frustrating. Trying to force someone to open up before they're ready will only lead to animosity from both parties. The best thing you can do is let your loved one know you're there for them and will listen in a non-judgmental manner when they're ready to talk.

Make a list of things to do as a family

Keeping your loved one's mind off the tragedy and improving their mood might be as modest as taking the kids to the park or taking a drive on the weekend. There are times when quiet time at a friend's cabin is preferable to a noisy rodeo with thousands of people there. Keep in mind that some activities and surroundings can exacerbate the symptoms of PTSD.

Ensure that your loved one receives the care they require

It's not uncommon for veterans suffering from PTSD to feel shame or embarrassment about their experiences, especially if they lost loved ones or were left with permanent disabilities. A person's suffering from PTSD is a sign of strength, not weakness. Offer to assist them in identifying resources and setting up appointments if they're open to it. You may also want to explore accompanying your family member to doctor's appointments if they agree. Family therapy is a highly underutilized, underrated intervention to facilitate healthy reintegration for everyone in the family impacted by PTSD.

Be a good listener

It's best not to force a person with PTSD to open up, but if they decide to do so, be sure to listen without interrupting or passing judgment. Let them know you're interested and concerned, but don't be afraid to provide suggestions. Listening carefully to your loved one is more important than what you say. Talking about the terrible experience may be necessary for someone who suffers from PTSD. Avoid telling your loved one to stop discussing the past and move on; opening up is part of the healing process. Instead, offer to talk as many times as they need. It's possible that some things your loved one says will be difficult for you to hear. Even if you don't agree with what they say, it's still necessary to show respect for their thoughts and feelings. Most people won't be as forthcoming if they see your tone as judgmental or condemning.

Mistakes to avoid in communication. ***Don't:***

- Give your loved one a simple answer or carelessly tell them everything will be fine
- Allow them to express their emotions or anxieties towards you uncontrollably
- Give unsolicited advice or tell your loved one what they should do

- Blame the PTSD for your family's ills, including your own
- Invalidate, diminish, or deny the terrible experience of your loved one
- Make threats or demands and issue ultimatums
- Make your loved one feel as if they are struggling more than others, which can lead to feelings of weakness
- Tell your loved ones how lucky they are that it wasn't worse
- Take control of the conversation by sharing your own personal stories or emotions

Care for your body and mind

As a caregiver to a loved one who suffers from PTSD, it is critical that you take care of yourself as well. Listening to traumatic stories or sharing in the experience of distressing symptoms like flashbacks might lead to the development of your own trauma symptoms. A traumatized person is more likely to feel exhausted and overwhelmed than a healthy person. You must nourish and care for yourself if you are going to be there for your loved one for the long-term and reduce your risk of secondary trauma. Some pointers for maintaining your own well-being:

- Maintain healthy sleep, exercise, and diet while also attending to any medical issues that may arise.
- Set up a network of people to help you out. Lean on your loved ones, trusted friends, a therapist or support group, or your religious community for help. Talking about what you're going through and how you're feeling can be quite therapeutic.
- Allow yourself time to live your life. Don't let go of the people, interests, and pastimes that bring you joy.

- Divvy up the burden. Allow yourself some time off by asking for support from family and friends. You might also look into local respite care options.
- Decide on ground rules. Recognize and accept your own unique set of strengths and weaknesses. It's important to understand your boundaries, convey them to the other people involved, and then follow through on those restrictions.

TOGETHER, DEVISE A STRATEGY FOR DEALING WITH A CRISIS

PTSD can cause symptoms like panic attacks and night terrors in your loved one. Before dealing with an emergency with a veteran, make sure you have a plan in place. Make sure your loved one has somewhere to go to calm down after a particularly upsetting recollection, and then make an appointment with a therapist or support group as soon as possible to make sure everything is okay.

Reduce your level of tension

Reducing the amount of tension in your home can help your loved one deal with trauma. Everyday rituals can help create a sense of familiarity and security at home. Don't invite anyone over who could potentially upset the veteran, even if unknowingly. As the person with PTSD tries to reintegrate into the family, it is helpful to avoid imposing too many demands or tasks on them.

Dealing with volatility and anger

Those suffering from PTSD may find it difficult to control their emotions and actions. Extreme irritation, depression, or furious outbursts are common symptoms as well as constantly being on edge, both physically and emotionally. Due to their inability to fall asleep on a regular basis, people who suffer from insomnia are more likely than others to respond emotionally and physically out of character when confronted with everyday stressors. Many people with PTSD use anger as a mask to hide other emotions such as loss, helplessness, or guilt. Instead of feeling weak and vulnerable, they feel powerful and in control when they are angry. Others struggle to keep their rage contained until it comes gushing out of nowhere.

If you notice a change in the behavior of your loved one when they're irritated, it could be a sign that they're becoming angrier. As soon as you see the first warning signs, take action to diffuse the situation. Here's advice on how to deal with rage or aggressive behavior:

- Timeouts can be called at any time by either of you. Decide on a timeout signal—a word or hand gesture—and stick to it.
- When someone requests a timeout, the conversation must halt immediately.
- Agree on the details of the timeout, such as where you'll be and what you'll be doing.

Whether or not you employ a timeout, consider these important tips:

- Keep your cool. Try to remain cool throughout an emotional outburst. It will do you a world of good to reassure a loved one that you are secure.
- Don't be a bother. Make sure you don't smother or grip the person. People who have been traumatized may feel in danger as a result.

- Ask if you can help in any way. What can I do for you at this moment? A break or a new location can also be suggested.
- Put your safety first—including making sure any children in the household are safe.
- Leave the house or lock yourself in a room if you can't calm the individual down despite your efforts. The police should be called immediately if you fear that your loved one is going to hurt himself or others.

Even though anger is normal, it can have major implications for a person's relationships, health, and state of mind when it is chronically and explosively out of control. Your loved one's rage can likely be managed with your help, but the root causes of the anger need to be found along with your loved one learning new ways to communicate their feelings.

When in doubt, seek emergency assistance

It's unfortunate, but PTSD can lead to crisis circumstances. As noted above—but worth repeating—if your loved one is threatening to hurt themselves or others, don't hesitate to get help. Call 911 to get your loved one to the hospital or bring the veteran to the hospital yourself if they'll cooperate.

Reconvening:

If you're taking a time out or other type of break from your loved one, don't dwell on your anger when you're taking that break. Instead, take some time to carefully plan out how you'll approach a constructive conversation when you reconvene, and come up with a solution. When you meet up again, make a pact with one another:

- You and your loved one should share ideas about how to solve the problem.
- Do not utter a word while the other individual is still expressing his or her thoughts.
- A statement such as "I think" or "I feel" is appropriate. Using the pronoun "you" can imply blame.
- Keep an open mind and listen. Don't point out the flaws in one another.
- Don't get bogged down in the details. Both of you are most likely to come up with good suggestions.
- Together, decide which solutions you'll implement.

If you're a family member or other close relation of a loved one with PTSD, hopefully this chapter has provided you insights and ideas to better communicate and cope with the challenges of your loved one.

Veterans are in charge of the next chapter, so if you're that family member/relation reading this, your loved one may appreciate if you now give the book back to them. In the middle of the chaos, the next chapter guides spiritual and religious veterans through the steps they need to take to rediscover their spirituality and find meaning again. It also teaches them how to use spirituality as a healing tool.

TRUSTING GOD THROUGH PTSD

WHAT DOES THE BIBLE HAVE TO SAY ABOUT PTSD?

WHILE THE BIBLE was written long before the term "posttraumatic stress disorder" came about, some of the Bible's indirect lessons provide a wealth of wisdom that can be useful and relevant if you have PTSD—especially if you're a Christian who grapples with combat-specific PTSD and coming to terms with the horrors you have been involved with and witnessed. Christians are acutely aware of God's high regard for human life and frequently experience intense guilt related to their involvement in war. If that's you, have faith—and read on. The need to remind yourself of God's love, forgiveness, and value cannot be overstated.

We've examined in prior chapters the types of "stressors" that can lead to PTSD. Exactly why some people develop PTSD while others do not is still a mystery. According to research, factors such as your genetic make-up, the sort of support you receive after a traumatic incident, and the presence of other life stresses may influence developing PTSD. Disturbingly, even while signs of PTSD normally appear soon after a trauma, this isn't always the case. PTSD can develop years later. And, some people suffer from PTSD for years, while others just need a few months to recover.

Combat-related PTSD appears to be distinct from other types of PTSD. Military personnel are frequently both the victim and the attacker in warfare, which complicates the situation. Your symptoms of combat-specific PTSD may include melancholy, guilt, hypervigilance, and low self-esteem. As a combat veteran, you may have a particularly difficult time coming to terms with the horrors you have witnessed, accepting your role in the conflict, and readjusting to civilian life. It can be especially difficult as a Christian to accept the taking of another's life, even as an act of war. Acutely aware of God's high regard for human life, you may experience intense guilt, even if the killing was necessary.

As a Christian combat veteran, you may have a more acute understanding of your own sinfulness than non-combatants do. Your military duty may make you feel unworthy of God's love. Accepting God's forgiveness might be especially challenging if you have PTSD. You may regret the choices you made in the many no-win scenarios in which you found yourself during conflicts. Your memories of the horrors of war may haunt you, and you may always be on high alert due to the months you spent living in dangerous settings. There is always a glimmer of optimism, however, no matter how dire things look. Hope comes from God; no other source can provide that which God can give you.

That's why, in addition to physical and psychological healing, spiritual well-being should also be addressed as part of the healing process. Counselors, doctors, family members, pastors, and others in your church can all be valuable resources in the healing process. Of course, God is the ultimate healer and counselor, and God is also your most crucial supporter. Psalm 61:2-3 by David reads, "From the end of the earth I call to you when my heart is faint. Lead me to the rock that is higher than I." Being a Christian means that you believe in God, read and study God's word, pray, and keep in touch with other Christians. When you are in trouble, you can turn to God for help and make good use of the tools God offers.

If you or someone you love has been diagnosed with PTSD, naturally it will take time to recover. "Thorn in the flesh" (2 Corinthians 12:7-10) has been likened to this. It's true that God offers to heal but only when and how God deems suitable. Until that time comes, God provides enough grace to get through the difficult times. Thorns hurt, and PTSD is a painful thorn. The good news is that you can keep going to God and remembering how trustworthy God has been in the past.

Coping with or overcoming PTSD requires a firm grasp of the truth. Again, the need to remind yourself of God's love, forgiveness, and value cannot be overstated. A person's self-worth is based on what God says about you rather than on what you have done or what has been done to you. You don't have to choose a side as a victim or an offender. If you have accepted Jesus Christ, then all of your sins have been forgiven; you have been sealed with the Holy Spirit, you have been redeemed by God (Romans 8:17, Ephesians 1:13-14, and 1 John 3:1-3), and you have been called beloved children (Romans 8:14–17; Ephesians 1:13–14; and 1 John 3:1–3) by God.

Yet, in the wake of the death of a loved one—such as a battle buddy in combat—you may believe that you are undeserving of being spared. However, in the face of "survivor's guilt," believe in God's sovereignty; believe that God has a plan for every person's life; and believe and have faith that those who died in a war or other calamity were loved every bit as much as those who made it through unscathed. For each individual, God has a certain plan in mind. In Ephesians 2:10, we learn that God has a plan for each of us and that he enjoys the time we spend on this earth. Understanding this can help you get rid of the idea that your life isn't worth living.

It's critical to surround yourself with people who are willing to extend mercy and forgiveness while also speaking the truth to you with love. It's equally critical that the people who care for you receive similar spiritual help. A strong relationship with your local church is essential. It is critical for both you and your loved ones to spend time with God in prayer and reading his word. It's also critical to practice self-care and engages in rejuvenating activities. PTSD can make you feel as if your life is being taken over by it. It is just as crucial to engage in activities that are fun and life-enhancing as it is to face PTSD head-on.

PTSD is a challenging condition to deal with. It's possible to yield to God's love, fight off the PTSD as best you can, and eventually rest in God's kindness. Hebrews 4:14–16 urges you to approach God confidently and to pour out your heart to him. In Romans 8:35–38, you are told that nothing can separate you from God's love. If you have PTSD, God has the ability to restore your mental wellness. Give thanks to God, our Savior's loving father and all-comforting God, who cares for you in your suffering and uses that compassion and consolation to comfort you and others. In the same way that we share in Christ's affliction, so do we share in our own comfort through Christ. (2 Corinthians 1:3–5)

WHAT DO YOU THINK JESUS WOULD SAY TO SOMEONE SUFFERING FROM PTSD?

A plethora of books have been written about Jesus' ability to be the ideal counselor. In most cases, they emphasize his ability to accept people for who they are, meet them where they are, and offer compassion when they are going through difficult times. They also point to the numerous instances in which he responded to inquiries by asking even more questions as evidence that he was an excellent listener. If Jesus were to walk the world today, what would he have to say to those who are suffering from PTSD? What do you suppose he would think of contemporary medical procedures and medications? He wouldn't even describe many experiences as traumatic. While you cannot exactly understand God's thoughts, you can use what has been revealed about Jesus' character throughout scripture to get a good notion of how he would respond to the suffering that you are experiencing as a victim of trauma in today's society. Consider the following four things that Jesus would say to those suffering from PTSD:

"I'm not bothered by your trauma in the least. To me, you aren't a broken person."

Even if you don't believe in God, most historians agree that the Bible is an historically accurate source. The history of the Israelites and the Christians is depicted in the Old and New Testaments. Their countries have been taken over and peoples taken into captivity again and again. It took two centuries for the northern Israeli tribes to be subjugated and taken captive by the Assyrians. A sequence of nineteen evil and pagan kings reigned over the northern tribes of Israel for almost 200 years. Short reigns were punctuated by assassinations, bloodshed, and brutality throughout the era. The Babylonians (586 B.C.), Persians (538 B.C.), Greeks (332 B.C.), Maccabees (164 B.C.), and Romans (63 B.C.) all followed this pattern. Beginning with the life of Jesus and work through the early Christian church's history, we see Jesus betrayed by one of his disciples, his agony, and his death on the cross. His disciples were assaulted, imprisoned, and executed. They also had to watch as their loved ones were tortured while they were still alive and killed. It wasn't an easy path to be a follower. According to today's mental health categories, these folks would have been subjected to trauma and presumably diagnosed with PTSD. Trauma is not a new phenomenon in the world, and Jesus' experience was no exception. He saw it all, whether during his own life on Earth or witnessing suffering in the lives of his people for millennia. On the other hand, Jesus is uniquely qualified to bear the weight of trauma.

"There's a silver lining to your injury. Your pain serves a greater purpose."

Trauma alters your personality. Period. However, a negative shift isn't required. Despite the fact that trauma is typically seen as the cause of a downward spiral, it's vital to remember that trauma may also propel you toward an incredible life transformation. This lesson was recently brought home to me in a profound way. My heart broke when a young woman, who had recently lost her father to a heart attack, stood up at a church meeting to pray for another young woman going through an abusive relationship. As she began to pray, she said something to the effect of:

"The worst of what we're going through here on Earth is the worst of what we'll ever go through. We only have to endure 80 or 90 years of this. And if that's the worst that we have to deal with, we're grateful due to the certainty of seeing you again in Heaven, where there is no pain or trauma. As a result, we turn to God for strength and comfort as we face this difficult moment. Use it to help us become more like Jesus, Lord!

My mind was blown. In the wake of the death of her father, this young lady was able to articulate an important truth: Trauma should be used to our advantage. It's supposed to help you rediscover what's important in life. Put aside selfishness and other things you've permitted in your life to replace God. Hopefully, it will help you become more like Christ. Remember that God tends to use those who have been hurt as his most effective leaders. All of Noah's friends and acquaintances were killed by a flood. As Abraham made his way up a mountain, he had to be ready to sacrifice his only son, Isaac. Joseph's own siblings deceived him and sold him into slavery. The list is endless. They all went on to become great leaders—and their experiences turned them into the leaders they needed to become. Some think the Bible is a story of people who persevered despite adversity.

"The scars remain so that they can tell a tale."

Trauma has a long-term effect on your life. It's not a minor cut that will heal itself and then fade away. Rather, it will leave a mark on your soul. Christians commonly use phrases like "restoration," "redemption," or "healing" when counseling people who have been traumatized. To someone who has experienced great loss, these words of comfort and consolation may seem off-putting, despite their biblical foundations. After what you've been through, how can you possibly expect to be restored, redeemed, or healed? But, trauma scars are meant to transform you. After a traumatizing encounter, the body's natural response is to release adrenaline. To say that an abnormal event might leave you unchanged may seem like stating the obvious, but it isn't. Following his resurrection,

Christ appeared to one of his disciples in John 20:24–29. Remember, this was only a short time after enduring the heinous agony of his crucifixion and death.

When Jesus initially appeared to the disciples, Thomas, one of the original twelve disciples, was absent. The others told him, "We have seen the Lord!" Thomas would not believe it unless he saw Jesus' nail imprints and was able to sink his own finger into the holes. A week later the disciples, including Thomas, were in a house and though the doors were locked, Jesus appeared and stood among them. "Put your finger here; see my hands," Jesus told Thomas. "Reach out your hand and put it into my side." Get over your skepticism and believe. Jesus told Thomas. In response, Thomas exclaimed, "My Lord and my God!" Jesus replied, "Blessed are those who have not seen and yet have believed."

Observe Jesus' scars, which haven't healed or faded away. They didn't leave. The marks of his anguish stayed on his body even after he had conquered death. Furthermore, it was because of these wounds that Thomas came to think about what he did. Don't you believe that Jesus, with all his might, could have rewarded himself with a brand new body? He could have done it, of course. Instead, Jesus' testimony was completed by the scars that remained. When your hand touches a scar on your body, you're likely reminded of what happened to cause it. Think of it as pressing a scar on your heart with your hand. Is there a story behind the scar? What's going to happen at the end? Nothing speaks more eloquently than the narrative of a person who has overcome adversity and is now living a life of purpose and strength. That kind of story can be yours via Jesus, who offers a way to get there.

"Rely on your doctors but keep your faith in me."

"To be healed, all you have to do is believe." Have well-meaning Christians ever told you this when you were going through a tough time? Though well-intentioned, this sentiment is unnecessarily simplistic. If they say, "Just go step off the edge of that cliff," you might as well take their advice then as well. In order to soar, what you have to do is believe in yourself! It's undeniable that faith is also an important factor in the healing process: Believe in yourself as well as in God! "The prayer of faith will save the sick" is in James 5:15. Jesus adds, "Your faith has made you whole" in Mark 5:34. Nevertheless, in Mark 2:17, Jesus says, "It is those who are sick who require a physician, not the healthy." He validates medicine as a part of human healing. An apostle of Jesus and a gospel writer himself, Luke was an expert in medicine. Medical science and religious belief are not adversaries. It's not a choice between the two. As a matter of fact, they are meant to work together.

Trauma inflicts physical, mental, and spiritual damage. In order for your wounds to truly heal, you must attend to every element of their care. Even if the healing can take place in the physical realm, it will always need spiritual elements to create a sense of well-being and tranquility. According to popular belief, fear has no place in a room where God is present. When a doctor has faith, he or she is able to entrust the patient's care to God. I have no doubt that he can likewise tap into the infinite knowledge and understanding of God. Give the discipline of science to medical science and the discipline of faith to God and his word. Because medicine isn't certain, faith and medicine are meant to operate together, so when it comes to rest and peace, rely on Jesus rather than your doctors.

Faith is predicated on embracing ambiguity. What science is unable to explain, faith fills in the blanks. This life is merely a gift from God, and you will meet Him face to face one day. Regardless of how irrational it may appear at any given time, faith assures us that God works all things together for his greater good. Having faith in a knowing God is not something you can buy or borrow. Faith is a gift from God—a gift that can provide hope and help you to remain in Jesus when all appears lost. Consider what Jesus might be saying to you as you seek to reconcile your faith with your trauma:

"I'm not bothered by your trauma in the least. To me, you aren't a broken person." . . . "There's a silver lining to your injury. Your pain serves a greater purpose. " . . ."The scars remain so that they can tell a tale." And, "Rely on your doctors, but keep your faith in me."

PTSD RECOVERY IS A LONG-TERM PROCESS

In an ideal world, we'd be able to guarantee a speedy recovery from PTSD. It can take a long time to get over a traumatic event, and each person's healing process is different. When it comes to PTSD, there is no one-size-fits-all treatment. In 2 Corinthians 12:7-8, the apostle Paul describes a "thorn" in his flesh, which he prayed for to be removed, but it never was. Nevertheless, his faith in a full recovery did not waver. In reading 2 Corinthians 12:9-10, Paul is clear that his grace is sufficient for you because of the perfecting of his strength in your weakness. In order for Christ's strength to rest on me, Paul says, "I shall thus boast all the more joyfully of my weaknesses." In other words, for the love of Christ, he is willing to put up with his own insufficiencies and those of others, as well as sufferings, persecution, and natural disasters. "As a result, I'm stronger when I'm at my weakest."

There is light, even in the darkest times of our lives. God's children can stand even when at their weakest because Christ lives within them. "Suck it up" isn't Paul's demand. He's reminding us that God's love and power aren't dependent on your health or ability, but rather that you are a vessel for wonderful, amazing things—regardless of how you value yourself. PTSD is a difficult condition to deal with. Avoid doing it alone. As important as are treatment, medication, and other forms of assistance, you must never lose sight of God's unwavering and unending love for you. Even if tragedy has broken the emotional bond between experiencing and understanding God's love, understand that God's love for you does not depend on your capacity to always experience it. Right now, he's there, holding you and protecting you in ways you may not be aware of.

As a child of God, you are complete in God's eyes (Romans 8:14-17; Ephesians 1:3-6; 1 John 3:1-3). God's opinion of you does not change when you need help to heal, no matter how devastating the situation (Romans 5). Whenever you cry out for aid or convey your feelings of anguish, God hears you. If you call out to him, he will respond with a loving hug and a kind word (Hebrews 4:14-16).

WHAT CAN CHRISTIAN COUNSELING DO FOR ME?

A Christian counselor with competence in treating complex PTSD can help Christians who are suffering from complex PTSD integrate secular psychological therapy with biblical wisdom. Including God in the healing process, even if it doesn't necessarily speed up the process, can provide tremendous consolation if you're dealing with C-PTSD. Counseling from a Christian perspective can be especially helpful if you have felt isolated and alone because of past trauma. Jesus can be brought into your sessions as a reminder that he understands and longs to help his children be free of their pain.

Interactive Questions:

- Do you have a sense of remorse about the deaths you caused during the conflict?
- Is it now clear to you that God loves you and doesn't hold it against you because you were part of his mission?
- Is there anything that you can do to begin the process of forgiving yourself and establishing yourself?
- God was always there for you, wasn't he?

The PTSD journey might be isolating at times, but it doesn't have to be. Remembering God's love and presence can help you get through the tough times.

Consider jotting down the questions above on a vision board or in your phone's notes app, so when needed, you can remember God's forgiveness and support.

Personally, the area of faith was the deepest wound for me in terms of the PTSD that I suffered. As far back as I can remember, God played a major role in my life. Even my very name! I was named after my two grandfathers, Harry and Albert. My grandfather Harry Cusack was a pastor. Growing up, my siblings and I lived with he and my grandmother for a short time, and I remember spending almost every day a church.

It became obvious to me later that from the beginning, God had a call out to me. However, I didn't answer that call until later. I'll get to that. When I was about 20 years old and a hospital corpsman stationed with the Marines, I met a friend, Lewis Hightower, at Marine Corps Recruit Depot, San Diego, and we were on the boxing team together. This brother was always at peace and regardless of any turmoil around him, it didn't seem to disturb his peace. When asking him about how he remained calm even in the most tumultuous situations, he would always respond with a Bible scripture: "The peace of God surpasses all understanding." From Lewis's testimony, I gained a better understanding of God's peace.

However, I later lost a grip on my faith when dealing with my PTSD issues. First, I blamed God, wondering how God could allow this to happen to me. Previously, when asked by my therapist or doctor if I'd lost hope, my response was always, "My hope is not in myself, but it is in God, and God would never fail me!" But, with PTSD I questioned my relationship with God. As I struggled with intrusive thoughts and nightmares, my faith began to wane. I asked God, "How did you allow this to happen to me?"

I was then walking one morning, and God responded, making me realize, "It didn't happen to me, but for me!" God's purpose for my life, and this book, is for me to help others dealing with similar issues. If I hadn't experienced what I did, I would have little understanding of what others suffer.

While I am a Christian, however, this book isn't meant to convert you, the reader. I respect whatever your faith or beliefs may be. The purpose of this book is to help as many people as possible who are dealing with PTSD and other military-related trauma. The time has come for you to reintegrate into society and reclaim your life—now that you are taking steps toward getting in tip-top condition.

Continue that journey in the following chapter.

RECLAIMING YOUR LIFE

RECOVERING FROM TRAUMA IN THERAPY CONSISTS OF THREE STAGES

Stage 1: Establishment of Safety

Assumptions about safety might be shattered by tragedy. It's something experts refer to as the detrimental impact you have on your own self-worth. Shame is the common source of fuel for this poor self-perception. According to experts, safety and trust are built early in life, but trauma can break those foundations. Restoring your basic sense of security and trust is the goal of the initial step in the PTSD recovery process. Your therapist will need to know about your past traumas, family background, and current relationships. The therapist's bond with you is crucial to the success of therapy. The therapist must make you feel at ease, so you may regain the trust and sense of safety that were shattered by the trauma.

In addition to taking a thorough medical history, tests and exams may be used to determine the extent of your dissociation and the severity of your PTSD. Collectively this critical intake will help you and your therapist evaluate the need for stability and decide on the speed and how to move toward the second stage, which will be remembrance and mourning. While you may want to get over this first period fast and get on with the healing process, safety and stability are essential for long-term recovery.

During this time, you and your therapist will begin developing coping mechanisms to help you feel less stressed—and more likely to stay inside your "window of tolerance." Falling outside your tolerance may cause you to feel triggered and overwhelmed by fear, anxiety, fury, or despair. This is when you'll be taught coping techniques such as picturing a safe and quiet place in your mind. Another method is to establish a box in your mind where you can store your memories and feelings until you are ready to revisit them. Only you have the key to open this box, which may be secured by a latch or a massive lock. Your personal preferences will decide the configuration of your box and its security.

Your therapist will help you discover the best ways for you to gain control over your emotions and memories, methods that will help you stay within your window of tolerance. The second stage of your rehabilitation, the empowerment to remember and mourn, begins once you've shown that you're ready to go deeper.

Stage 2: Remembrance and Mourning

When a survivor creates a new mental "schema" for interpreting what happened, the trauma can finally be over. The therapist listens to your tale of trauma in Stage 2. While you may describe traumatic experiences with few feelings, an incomplete recollection of events, or a sequence of motionless images, putting words or feelings into memory is critical, so go ahead and do it if you can. You may be able to identify the physical feelings you're experiencing.

It's up to you how much sorrow, guilt, and shame you're willing to face. It takes a lot of guts to open up about your experiences and be willing to face them, and telling your tale may cause you to experience unpleasant feelings. The tactics you learned in Stage 1 will come in handy to help you feel secure during the process of remembering. There is a chance, however, that the Stage 1 primary goal of establishing a level of safety may need to be reassessed during this second phase so that you remain within your window of tolerance.

Feeling protected and confronting the past must be balanced. It's up to you and the therapist to decide how fast or slowly you work. You can move back and forth between these first two stages and the next third stage of rehabilitation as many times as they like without encountering any time restrictions. Many parts of your traumatic memory are involved, including feelings of humiliation, remorse, powerlessness, sensations such as a constriction in your throat, and the image that depicts the horrific event in your mind. The neurological system may hold onto some of these memories.

Even if you've shared your experience many times, you may still be plagued by flashbacks, nightmares, or a generalized anxiety disorder. Because you may have been blamed for the terrible events, you may experience a moral sense of guilt or responsibility. You may need to rethink your prior world views, such as "It's not safe," "I am helpless," or "I can't trust anyone," and consider a new outlook so you'll feel more connected to your world, yourself, and your relationships.

Having a healthy working relationship with your therapist is essential. In the midst of a stressful situation, it is important to have someone who is empathetic and nonjudgmental. At long last, you're being heard! If the trauma is one of shame and guilt, you may also benefit from working with your counselor to create a new narrative about it. This can enable you to let go of guilt over what's transpired. Your self-esteem improves. You're ready to start relating to the people around you.

As challenging as Stage 2 can be, *persistence is a must*. Progress may include steps backward, and it may be difficult to notice progress, but trust that you are progressing! When you've finished this stage, you'll need to start over and work toward goals for the future. Stage 3 of the rehabilitation process is where this all takes place. This is going to be difficult—but liberating.

Stage 3: Reconnection

By this point, you've likely spent some time lamenting the loss of your old self, but you're now ready to begin creating a new one. Psychologist and psychoanalyst Erik Homburger Erikson developed the "Eight Stages of Psychosocial Development," which are characterized by a sense of self-determination, initiative, competence, identity, and intimacy. The trauma has a big impact on all of these, which is why healing is so difficult. Identity and intimacy concerns are especially a focus of treatment in this Stage

3. That's why spending time focusing on self-care is essential during this final phase, including taking good care of your health, your surroundings, your material requirements, and your relationships with others. This may include forming new types of relationships now that your old ones have been dismantled. Reconnecting with yourself and others is the goal.

You may want to go over some of the safety considerations you made in the first stage again in this stage. Reconnecting with others may require you to rediscover your sense of safety. The ability to explore earlier ambitions and dreams is now available. This is a chance to reimagine your identity. You have the opportunity now to embrace the best parts of your personality, which become key parts of your new identity. You should also forgive yourself, ridding yourself of guilt over a trauma event beyond your control. The experience may have helped you gain confidence in your self-defense abilities, but if you were assaulted, self-defense training could be an option to increase confidence.

During Stage 3 of the healing process, the trauma should have faded away, and there should be no more impediments to connection. There is a chance, however, that your recovery is not complete, and symptoms of PTSD can return during times of stress. When that happens, it's important to remember the coping mechanisms you developed in treatment to help you take care of yourself and remain within your window of tolerance. As a precaution, when symptoms pop up, you may want to go back to your therapist for a session or two. As a result of your help-seeking behavior, you have learned to take action!

CASE EXAMPLE: A PTSD SUFFERER'S JOURNEY THROUGH THE STAGES OF RECOVERY

What follows is a therapist taking us through an actual case of guiding a PTSD sufferer through the three stages:

Stage 1: Establishment of Safety

"I will get a thorough history from every PTSD sufferer I meet so that I can determine what they require in terms of safety and stabilization. There is the possibility that the person will feel disconnected from their immediate surroundings or their own sentiments. To put it another way, they may not be able to tell whether or not they are in danger at any given time. Jane (not her real name) showed up for an interview with a lot of nervousness. She was baffled as to the source of her uneasiness. When she mentioned a couple of instances that were considered distressing, I went back in time to learn more.

"While her father was a heavy drinker, she remembered growing up in an abusive household where her mother was aloof and cold. Her parents didn't make her feel loved at all, which started with her being sexually molested by the next-door neighbor when she was just five years old.

"To address instances of Jane not feeling safe, we worked together to discover ways for her to take care of herself. For example, I shared some 'window of tolerance' ideas. Among the go-to's that Jane developed were a riverside "calm place"; a wooden box with a latch; and a sleep-aid technique she dubbed 5-4-3-2-1. Some of these worked but only under certain conditions. To establish if Jane was ready for the next stage, I used a readiness scale.

"Jane didn't feel overwhelmed and thought she had the tools necessary to continue to the next step—but she was afraid because she would have to address the sorrow and guilt she had hidden."

Stage 2: Remembrance & Mourning

"Jane had a more difficult time with Stage 2. Her recollections were hazy and devoid of any sense of language or emotion. At this point, she was tasked with identifying common threads in her experiences. In her analysis, she was able to categorize these concerns as belonging to the adolescent years. When she was finally able to label her recollections as PTSD, it was a life-changing moment for her. She was able to connect the dots between her present-day actions, feelings, and thoughts and their origins in her history.

"After a while, Jane was able to distinguish the feelings that accompanied the physical sensations she was experiencing. Visualization and images in treatment sessions allowed her to focus on her body experiences and describe them in language. She recalled being abused sexually as a child, around the age of ten. It happened one time. Then, in her early twenties, she was sexually assaulted by an unknown assailant. She was also subjected to emotional abuse in her family.

"Together, Jane and I came to a decision about the best way to handle the situation. Almost a year went by before everything was finished. She was no longer plagued by dreams and no longer reacted to her triggers with a sense of being overwhelmed. She no longer experienced as much immobility in acting upon things as she had in the past. She also began to experience happiness in her life."

Stage 3: Reconnection

"Stage 3 was difficult for Jane because she had to entirely let go of her idea that she would never be secure or trust anyone. She felt she had no control over her own destiny. For her to begin socializing, we devised a series of steps to grow her comfort level. Her goal was to build her sense of safety over time, and she went back to tactics learned in Stage 1 to do this.

"Jane had a hard time pinpointing the qualities of her personality she liked. In her mind, she was also unworthy of any kind of romantic connection. She feared that her inability to fully participate in a relationship would harm others. Her unfavorable self-perceptions were challenged using a cognitive-behavioral method. This allowed her to progressively be able to believe that she was strong, courageous, and someone who persevered.

"After a while, Jane was able to form relationships with others. She gradually built up a network of women's retreats, Facebook pals, and online dating services to help her cope with her loneliness. As long as she didn't get too carried away, these methods worked for her.

"Jane had to briefly return to Stage 2 when fresh memories from her past surfaced and she felt overwhelmed, before moving forward again to Stage 3. However, as with going back to Stage 1 for safety techniques, each time we went back to a previous stage, it was much easier and less emotionally taxing than the prior time.

"After going through these three stages, for the first time in fifteen months, Jane felt happy and confident about her future."

The more you apply these steps, the faster and more efficient you will become at overcoming any situation you face.

PERSONAL GROWTH AFTER TRAUMA

Experiencing a difficult incident might help you grow as a person in the following ways:

Relating to others

Social support and interactions with others in the immediate aftermath of traumatic experiences, such as a car accident, war zone deployment, significant sickness, or bereavement, are key determinants of psychological recovery. Difficult times can strengthen your relationships with loved ones and allow you to see how much others care about you. You may come to value your relationships more and learn that you can rely on others to listen, care, and assist you when needed. Of course, when loved ones break your trust or are unsupportive, it may have the reverse impact, causing you to feel more alone and undeserving of love. New relationships can sometimes be formed through counseling, spiritual work, or groups like Alcoholics Anonymous. It is possible to learn that some people can be trusted, despite the fact that others can't.

New Possibilities

It has also been found that trauma can motivate you to engage in new activities, habits, and/or relationships that enhance your quality of life. An example is volunteering or advocating for change in communities that have been affected by traumatic events. A victim of rape, for example, might volunteer at a rape crisis organization. Experiences can be documented in writing or other forms of creative expression. Such activities may help you gain a sense of empowerment, wholeness, and connection as you meet new people and expand professional and/or social networks. You may experience a state of flow where you are both engaged and pushed by turning emotional anguish into useful work.

Personal Strength

It is possible as a survivor of traumatic events to lose your self-esteem as a result of your injuries or a belief that you did something wrong to deserve such harsh treatment. Self-blame for parental neglect or abuse, for example, may continue into adulthood for children. You may not have learned how to protect yourself emotionally or physically due to the lack of protection you received from your parents. In order to begin to recover, you must realize that you are not to blame for your own abuse. By confronting your traumas, you might discover your inner strength and the limits of your endurance. When you have a personal goal, you may find that you can be surprisingly strong when faced with bad memories and feelings.

Spiritual Change

In difficult times you may choose to view life-altering events, such as traumatic experiences, as a spiritual message that will help you adjust your life path. Your faith might be strengthened by realizing that you have little control over some elements of your destiny and may need to turn to a higher power for guidance. Researchers discovered that religion hastens rehabilitation by providing people with a sense of purpose as well as a sense of belonging among a caring and active community. A new outlook on life can be gained through prayer or meditation, allowing you to be more accepting of the present moment and hopeful about the future. Spirituality goes beyond religion. Although religion is popular, faith and spirituality carry power in the human mind.

A New Appreciation of Life

Following a traumatic experience, you may feel newfound gratitude for the life you've been given. Reconnecting with simple joys like nature walks and quality time spent with loved ones can help you heal from life's main stresses. Realizing how close you might have been to death, whether literally or spiritually, might make you not only grateful but allow you to use lessons learned from the trauma to do better in the future. You may look to rebuild your life. For some, becoming a parent especially offers a fresh start.

HERE ARE SOME TIPS TO HELP YOU GET BACK ON YOUR FEET AFTER PTSD:

Bear in mind that your past does not define who you are

Trauma has a lasting effect on your mind and body. This is understandable, given what you have seen and experienced. The thought of having to endure acts of violence, natural disasters, or war is utterly repulsive. Keep in mind that you are not defined by your past. The brain is capable of replacing traumatic events that had a profound impact on your life. Be present in the here and now. Keep your mind focused on the present by studying meditation, prayer, or spirituality. You can do it.

Allow yourself and others to be forgiven for past wrongs and resentments

This is a challenging task, especially if you have been directly affected by violence. When you can let go of your resentment and bitterness, you can make room for something greater in your life. Forgiveness is all about you, not about the other person; the reason you should forgive someone is that *you* deserve it. Angry and resentful feelings harm you more than the person who committed the wrongdoing. My friend, it's time to let go of the negative.

Make self-love and self-care a priority

Taking care of your body and mind is, of course, a terrific way to treat yourself. Take care of your physical and mental well-being by engaging in activities such as exercise, meditation, a healthy diet, and so on. Mindfulness meditation has been found to be helpful for those with PTSD, especially troops in conflict. Numerous studies have shown that practicing mindfulness can lower stress levels. In addition, experts believe that it can be useful for soldiers who are under high stress during combat.

Replace negative and destructive beliefs with new empowering ones

Negative thoughts can be replaced with positive ones to help you feel better about yourself. It's normal to be dubious of new ideas at first, but if you continue to introduce new ways of thinking, it ultimately becomes second nature. When a negative thought comes to mind, simply think or speak the opposite of it. There is a reciprocal relationship between positive words and thoughts. Replacing negative thinking may take time and effort, but the results can be long-lasting. Again, meditation may also be helpful.

 A thousand-mile trip begins with one step.

— LAO TZU

Take baby steps to effect subtle changes

This is a lovely quote—especially for individuals who have experienced trauma—and good to memorize. The healing process will not be immediate while dealing with traumatic events. As you wait for the process to unfold, be gentle with yourself. It's critical to practice self-compassion. You've been through enough.

Stay in touch with your friends and family

You can lose your ability to trust others after a terrible incident makes you feel alone in the world. And, while you may try not to bother others with your problems, it's often impossible to keep others from getting "infected" or burdened by your troubles if you isolate yourself. When possible, see people face-to-face rather than relying just on email or phone. Your stress hormones will be reduced if you have face-to-face contact with other people, as well as if you get physical affection and reassurance from them.

Obtain the necessary practical assistance

If you're unable to work or take care of your family because of illness or injury, don't be afraid to ask for help. Even if it's only running errands to relieve some stress, friends and family are likely to leap at the chance to help.

Express yourself verbally

Though wallowing in self-pity isn't a good idea, it's important to express how you're feeling about what's happened. If you're struggling with feelings of shame, rage, grief, or guilt, it may be difficult to voice them, but suppressing them will only make things worse. You may be able to share your feelings with a close friend or family member, but a mental health counselor who specializes in PTSD therapy is the ideal option.

Get back into a routine

As soon as you're able, try to get back into a pattern that is as similar to your former one as possible, though this is not totally necessary if you find a new routine that is a better fit for you. Routine will provide you a feeling of direction in your everyday activities—and allow you to make new, happy memories as well. If you've been injured physically, you may have to adapt to new constraints as you heal.

Be kind to yourself

Be realistic about your expectations of your ability to bounce back from a traumatic experience. Every experience you have, good or bad, has an impact on you. Putting too much pressure on yourself to "get better" in a set time frame is a waste of time. Find your inner power by facing your fears, challenging your inner critic, and becoming more aware of yourself. There's no due date for this process or expiration date for the results.

Do your best to surround yourself with positive people who will help you heal and start a new life

Those who have been through horrific circumstances need to be surrounded by people who are cheerful and upbeat. Those who know you've been through a traumatic incident should support you and not judge you. Don't be with people who are going to make it harder for you to make the adjustment. In a pessimistic society, negativity feeds on itself. When those with a bad attitude show up, avoid or simply ignore them. There are a lot of wonderful people around you who can help you become better.

To be free of personal tragedy requires accepting that suffering is a part of life. This is when you're most likely to grow.

As with every experience, you can benefit and grow from what you've been through. Even if it doesn't feel like that at times, what you've been through has likely strengthened you—not weakened you. In spite of how helpless and hopeless you may feel at times, recognize the incredible strength and courage within yourself.

Interactive Element:

- Have you gone through the stages of PTSD recovery?
- Which research data most intrigues you and why?
- Which steps would you prioritize in reclaiming your life following PTSD?

I'll provide you with actionable ideas in the following chapter to assist you in maintaining your recovery and avoiding relapse.

WHEN WOUNDS ARE REOPENED —MAINTAINING YOUR RECOVERY

PTSD RETRAUMATIZATION

IF YOU'VE RECOVERED from PTSD, there remains a chance that you become retraumatized when exposed to certain people, places, events, situations, and/or environments that trigger flashbacks of past trauma as if it were new. A retraumatizing experience might bring back unpleasant memories or even cause unsettling flashbacks. This type of event can be exceptionally strong in recreating the intense dynamics connected with the initial traumatic occurrences. Vivid flashbacks can especially be startling and alarming. Even though it's a complicated condition, medication and a positive outlook can help alleviate symptoms.

It's important not to confuse retraumatization with revictimization, in which you are subjected to the same kind of abuse or injury over and over again. Retraumatization doesn't directly injure you but triggers vivid memories, eliciting reactions similar to the original trauma but without repeating the exact traumatic events. Some retraumatizing experiences may involve physical or emotional pain. What makes them so potent is their ability to bring up memories that are painful if you have PTSD.

CAUSES OF RETRAUMATIZATION

Catastrophes such as natural disasters, wars, and terrorist acts can be abrupt, shocking, and devastating—and potential causes of retraumatization. You may find these scenarios frightening and evocative, even if your earlier experiences were in no way connected. Likewise, you may be retraumatized by a movie, TV show, or news that brings back traumatic recollections.

Witnessing domestic violence or child abuse could be a trigger if you are unable to intervene. Additionally, retraumatization may be triggered by an interaction with someone seen as a threat in a setting where physical danger appears to be present; this could include the person responsible for the original trauma being nearby. Even if you have not been physically abused or hurt, it can be enough to bring back terrible memories in an incredibly distressing way. Another probable source of retraumatization is a dysfunctional or violent relationship. Disagreements and abuse, no matter how far removed from the original event, can be powerful triggers for PTSD sufferers. If the prior trauma involves the loss of a loved one in a tragic way, that too may trigger retraumatization.

EFFECTS OF RETRAUMATIZATION ON MENTAL HEALTH

If you have PTSD, you know that even as treatment improves your PTSD, triggering circumstances can bring back terrible memories. Fortunately, there's a good chance that the coping mechanisms you developed to deal with symptoms, as well as perspectives you've gained, will still be useful. But retraumatization is a real obstacle in the recovery process because of the severity of the reaction it can create. Retraumatization can have the following effects on your mental well-being:

- Loss of self-assurance and security
- Pessimism, fatalism, and cynicism
- Dreams and memories more vivid than usual
- Consistent anxiety or paranoia that causes increased vigilance
- Agoraphobic behavior, i.e. fear of leaving your home or other safe place
- Increased sensitivity to triggers—reacting more forcefully or responding to more of them
- Increased susceptibility to various psychiatric or behavioral health problems due to increased stress responsiveness
- Increase in self-harm, including suicide attempts
- Hallucinations or delusions from reliving retraumatized emotions

In addition, retraumatization can influence the expression and development of other mental health disorders that often accompany PTSD, including:

- Substance use disorders: A comprehensive study found that nearly half of those with PTSD also had substance abuse conditions.
- Major depression: More than half of those with PTSD are also depressed.
- Other anxiety disorders: Those with PTSD often have anxiety disorders like obsessive-compulsive disorder, panic disorder, social anxiety, generalized anxiety disorder, and specific phobias.
- Eating disorders: In a study of women who sought help for eating problems, 52% had symptoms linked to PTSD.

Even while you may not forget the PTSD coping mechanisms you were taught, retraumatizing experiences can cause your recovery to falter for at least a short time. That makes returning to individual counseling and/or peer support groups important during these times.

EFFECTS OF RETRAUMATIZATION ON PHYSICAL HEALTH

Chronic stress can cause or make worse many medical problems, including those noted below, and in general PTSD is linked to these issues, with retraumatization possibly exacerbating them:

- Digestive disorders
- Loss of reproductive system functioning
- Cardiovascular disease
- Insomnia
- Chronic pain
- Respiratory disorders
- Arthritis
- Diabetes

RECOVERY FROM RETRAUMATIZATION AND PTSD

If you are retraumatized, you are more likely to rely on avoidance methods to shield yourself from memories of your trauma. However, this is the wrong strategy. While you might become pessimistic and disillusioned about recovering due to retraumatization, that's exactly when treatment is more critical than ever to continue moving forward. You must trust that therapies and coping mechanisms will work; there's no need for you to go back to square one by giving in. Long-term behavioral or mental health illness may increase your chance of relapse, but the frequency of relapse should never be used as a reason to give up. Focus on the future, and keep hope and positive feelings in mind during therapy for PTSD, even though relapses may occur.

You may benefit from intensive outpatient treatment—or even a hospital stay—with treatment from professionals who understand the obstacles and distractions that can sometimes sabotage your PTSD recovery progress. This can help you rededicate yourself to healing in a safe setting as you learn—or relearn—preventative practices and how to avoid the excessive reactions that lead to retraumatization. There's not a one-size-fits-all approach to PTSD treatment, and short-term setbacks can be overcome if there is a strong desire to get better—together with patience and self-acceptance.

THE IMPORTANCE OF ONGOING, LONG-TERM PTSD TREATMENT

Due to the limitations of short-term treatments, you may be unable to find a way to recover from your condition. A long-term PTSD treatment program can provide the more specific type, quality, and length of care you need to learn to live again and reclaim your feelings of joy, trust, and confidence after PTSD.

LIMITS OF SHORT-TERM THERAPY

As you attempt to cope with the overwhelming emotions brought on by your trauma, the mental processes associated with PTSD often show up as concrete behavioral symptoms. It is common, in these instances, to retreat from normal activities including school, work, and socializing. People and things that once seemed harmless might now be triggering for you—even connections with those closest to you. If the original trauma occurred during a vulnerable time in your life, such as the transition into adulthood, these types of setbacks might be more likely.

Outpatient and short-term PTSD treatment cannot always address the full spectrum of your unique circumstances, including retraumatization and functional difficulties, or you may receive poor or ineffective treatment, resulting in you being unable to experience sustained recovery in certain circumstances. Hence, seeking the best available care in the most appropriate setting is paramount so as not to demoralize you and worsen your trauma.

THE ART OF SURVIVING

When short-term treatments fall short, a new ray of hope for more permanence in your PTSD recovery can be found in a lengthier treatment period. The advantages include:

- **Building a Therapeutic Alliance**: A therapist-client relationship takes time to develop, and this is especially true if you've been traumatized and retraumatized. A longer-term PTSD program allows you to build trust with

your therapist, so you start talking about what make you feel bad.
- **Offering Breadth and Depth**: Short-term treatment may not address the full breadth and depth of your trauma, whereas longer treatment allows you to better deal with all of the complicated ways in which trauma and retraumatization have impacted your life.
- **Building Skills:** Symptoms, including nightmares and overt emotional problems, tend to be the focus of short-term PTSD treatment, but it's typical with PTSD to be plagued by considerably more basic behavioral issues. You must develop the practical skills necessary to regain your sense of self-worth, form new friendships, and engage in normal daily activities without fear or anxiety, in addition to addressing the underlying causes of your trauma. The more time you spend in long-term therapy, the more comprehensively these emotional and behavioral needs can be addressed, allowing you to become more self-reliant and sociable, have a healthy sense of self-worth, and create goals in life.
- **Experiencing a Safe Space**: In order to avoid retraumatization that could impede your recovery, you may need to isolate yourself from your normal surroundings for an extended length of time. In long-term residential therapy, the distractions and triggers of daily life are limited, so you can focus exclusively on your recovery. Having by your side physicians and others who understand and affirm your thoughts, feelings, and personal experiences may be a very empowering experience. When someone tells you, "Your sentiments are valid," it can be a huge step in the healing process.
- **Recovering as a Family**: It's not only you that suffers from PTSD; it affects your entire family. If your family has been

a part of your retraumatization, having the time and support to heal together is priceless. True healing for everyone needs to happen in a safe place where you can talk about your shared experiences and learn how to work both individually and together.

Again, recovering from PTSD is not one-size-fits-all, and short-term treatment may not be enough to help you recover. You need the right kind, quality, and length of treatment to meet your individual needs. Whether short- or long-term, the recovery process is a journey—but it's one that you can start *now*, if you haven't already. Embark on this journey—and have confidence in your ability to achieve a real and lasting recovery to get back your feelings of joy, independence, and trust so that you can live a richer, more satisfying life, the one you want for yourself.

MY PARTING THOUGHTS

I hope this book has given you insights into better understanding your PTSD, provided you coping techniques for overcoming challenges, brought you new ideas for therapies, healing, and recovery, and will help your personal relationships and self-fulfillment grow in leaps and bounds. But most of all, my strongest wish is that I have given you hope. You are among so many of us that have been through this and have prevailed. You, too, can do it.

I'm rooting for you!

CONCLUSION

To my active duty, reserve, and veteran brothers, sisters, their families, and friends, I highly recommend that to recover from PTSD you avail yourselves of the many services offered free of charge to you—because you earned them through your service to our country. This includes services through the VA. When you come back from a war zone, you are not the same person who deployed. PTSD and military trauma are rightfully named traumas, and they change your life. However, experiencing them doesn't mean your life is over.

George Washington, the founding father of this great country, understood the need for treatment for PTSD sufferers. He fought, albeit unsuccessfully, for funding from Congress. Much later in our country's history, other U.S. presidents saw the critical need for PTSD treatment for soldiers and helped establish facilities that led to the creation of VA Medical Centers. So, the services are there—established for *your* benefit. Use them to get the treatment you deserve. But take heart and do not be discouraged if you have a less than pleasant experience at any given time with a receptionist, administrator, therapist, physician, or the like. The right, caring professionals exist to help you—even if you have to seek further among the options.

In this book, I mention a variety of therapy options. Different people find different therapies effective. Work with your therapist to find out which methods work best for you. Remember, all therapy methods described in this book are scientifically proven to help veterans recover from PTSD, but each addresses PTSD in a different way. Do not give up until you find the right combination that works for you. There is always hope. With the help of these therapies, I have overcome my PTSD, and so can you!

Finding a new purpose in life can also help you overcome PTSD. Writing this book to help other PTSD sufferers has helped me understand and more fully overcome my own PTSD. Just like me, you need to find your purpose, something that you feel passionate about. Finding your WHY could be the key to changing your life. Whatever it is that motivates you is the first key to finding your WHY. I hope this book might help begin your journey to finding that meaningful WHY in your life.

I especially pray and hope that this book will help you overcome your PTSD, and that you will be able to transform your life to live a happier and more rewarding life. God bless!

APPENDIX I: PTSD THOUGHT LEADERSHIP INTERVIEWS

PTSD Thought Leadership Viewpoints: Interviews with Mental Health Professionals on Pressing Challenges, Opportunities, and/or Advice Facing Those with PTSD

Below are thoughts and excerpts from a series of interviews I did with professionals well-versed in helping veterans coping with PTSD struggles.

Navy Corpsman:

Joe is a retired Navy Corpsman who served with the Marine Corps. His 20 years of service included two combat tours in Iraq. Joe suffered from PTSD for several years before receiving treatment. He now works at a VA (Veteran Affairs) hospital as a PEER Support specialist helping veterans dealing with PTSD and other mental health issues.

When asked about the biggest complaint heard among veterans during his group therapy sessions, Joe responded, "The VA doesn't recognize marijuana medication therapy." As to changes the VA could make to serve veterans better? Joe answered, "Better follow-up and continuation of services after discharge." He also suggested that it would be great if the VA could set up gathering places for vets to tell their stories, such as coffee socials. Lastly, Joe relayed this message to combat veterans: "Recognize you will not be who you were before, but you can become a better version of yourself."

Chaplain Robinson:

Chaplain Robinson works at a VA medical center and was also a chaplain with my unit. He pointed out an interesting concept that is spoken of more nowadays. When addressing PTSD, he breaks it into two components: moral injury and PTSD. Moral injury relates to your identity and how you view yourself. A goal in addressing moral injury is to help you develop decisional forgiveness, i.e. learn to deconstruct the negative façade you may have in believing that you violated your morals. PTSD, on the other hand, relates to dealing with your symptoms, rather than your identity.

One of the main issues the chaplain hears from veterans is, "I can't seem to forget," which in turn leads to repressed feelings and avoidance of situations that bring reminders of traumatic experiences. Chaplain Robinson suggests that the VA can best help veterans by having highly trained staff.

His message to you as a veteran is to think of the care you are seeking as like eating an elephant: Take one bite at a time. You are your best advocate, so also take control and be assertive in your own care. "Don't give up, don't quit; you are still a warrior," says the chaplain. He relays this quote by JT Cooper: "If they didn't kill you over there, don't let them kill you here!" Finally, Chaplain Robinson suggests the book, Care For The Sorrowing Soul, by Duane Larson and Jeff Zust, and that veterans check out this website: www.honoringthecode.com

Tammy, Nurse Practitioner:

Tammy is a nurse practitioner at a VA medical center and was also previously my nurse manager in the VA's Mental Health unit where I worked. Tammy stated that most veterans complain of feeling weak, remorseful, guilty, and irritable. Tammy believes that professionals can help our veterans more by developing better dialog with them.

If you have PTSD, or think you might, her suggestions for improving your situation are:

- Call the VA in your area
- Go to the VA
- Ask specifically for PTSD services
- Ask for a diagnostic assessment

Tammy added that treatment is the best resource for dealing with PTSD.

Scott, Nurse Manager:

Scott is a nurse manager of Nursing Education at the VA. He was also an Army staff sergeant, having served for 10 years. Scott's suggestion for VA staff is to "Meet veterans where they are [in the process of recovery from PTSD] and build from there." Scott's suggestion to you as a veteran is to reach out to the VA because the resources are there; there are people that want to help; and you don't have to fight PTSD or military trauma alone. If you aren't receiving services from the VA, he urges, "Don't be afraid to ask for help. Go to enrollment and eligibility and sign-up."

Amy. Mental Health Therapist:

Amy, a mental health therapist, LISW-S at the VA, finds that most veterans suffering from PTSD after returning from service are upset and uncertain about whether their value system—with clarity of right from wrong—was abandoned during service to do their jobs as ordered. The sense of self becomes conflicted and guilt-ridden, with a reduction in self-esteem. Shame or fear of appearing weak makes it difficult to acclimate to families/loved ones or get help, a dynamic that prompts isolation, depression, and a cycle that perpetuates self-degradation. This cycle also leads to feeling "stuck," no longer serving—but no longer fitting into civilian life.

Amy suggests the VA as a safe space for healing, though due to an inadequate number of frontline clinicians, care might not be prompt or with adequate frequency or duration. While referrals to mental health counselors in your local community are possible, those resources are also often backed up or insufficient. Evidence-based therapies are always good practice, but having some therapeutic flexibility may be required to get the best individual outcome for you.

"The stigma of mental health care combined with feeling 'weak' when diagnosed with PTSD requires more support, more education, and more protocol upon discharge so our veterans do not suffer in a prolonged manner on their own," says Amy. "Our VA facilities need to be safe places for healing and visualized as a necessary component to serving. Our goal of reducing veteran suicide will only occur when we invest appropriately in veterans' mental health care."

To the individual veteran Amy says, "Be willing to recognize that getting care is not a weakness but an opportunity to get care, so you can return to your family in a healthy, loving manner. The best way to access the resources available to you is to start with whoever you trust, then go to a specialized facility to meet your further needs in a safe place."

Amanda Held, Founder of H.O.O.V.E.S:

Amanda Held, the founder of H.O.O.V.E.S (Healing Of Our Veterans through Equine Services), has served in the Air Force National Guard as a first sergeant. Amanda struggled with PTSD for a time, but after overcoming her major struggles with it, became intent on helping others suffering from PTSD, and she created the HOOVES program. This program is set up as a four-day retreat. At the time of this writing, the program is offered at no cost to its attendees—as the costs are absorbed by donors.

Author's Note: This program is amazing and believe me when I tell you it's life-changing! I attended the program for the first time in 2019, after a soldier from my unit told me about HOOVES (p.s. thank you, Sarah!). Through that experience, I acquired the tools to deal with my residual PTSD problems. I completed another retreat in 2022 as an alumnus. Again, I was amazed by the additional coping tools given at this retreat.

The HOOVES retreat involves equine-assisted facilitation along with in-classroom studies, yoga, aromatherapy, meditation, breathwork, massage therapy, and chiropractic therapy. The classroom studies are based on neuro-linguistic programming—a method of helping you identify negative thoughts and behaviors and replacing them with positive thoughts and behaviors.

Amanda believes the most common issue veterans face is: "Being able to fit back into civilian society. HOOVES, she says, can teach you as a veteran how to understand your blueprint (purpose), so you can realize you're not wrong—and neither is anyone else. It's dealing with a fundamental conflict of values.

Amanda suggests that you may need to learn that you aren't the same person you were prior to the military—but you can learn to rebuild your life in support of who you are today. She named three keys to post-traumatic growth:

1. Discovering your blueprint: asking yourself what your strengths are
2. Identifying how your challenges have sharpened your strengths
3. Putting your pain into your purpose: "Make your mess, your message."

As new information is learned, Amanda incorporates into the HOOVES retreat. She also recommended these books to all veterans dealing with PTSD:

- The Value Factor, by Dr. John DeMartini
- Loving What Is, by Bryon Katie

As noted above, the cost of the HOOVES retreat, which runs about $2,200 per person, is covered by donations from sponsors—and offered free to participants. The cost of airfare for those coming from out of state has also typically been covered. The HOOVES website is noted in Appendix B, among other veteran PTSD resources listed.

APPENDIX II: ADDITIONAL RESOURCES

PTSD sufferers can benefit from the following helpful resources.

Department of Veterans Affairs:

https://www.va.gov/: It is the mission of the Department of Veterans Affairs (VA) to help veterans and their families through various programs and services. Programs include: education and rehabilitation services, compensation for military-related impairments or deaths, home loan guarantees, pensions, burials, and health care including the services of nursing homes, clinics, and medical facilities. Health care services for eligible war veterans are provided at 170 VA medical centers and outpatient clinics across the country. In addition to health care, non-health care benefits include disability compensation, vocational rehabilitation, education help, house loans, and death insurance. There are 135 national cemeteries available for soldiers and their families to use for burial and commemoration.

Acronym: VA
Website: Department of Veterans Affairs (VA)

Contact: Contact the Department of Veterans Affairs
Local Offices: Find Facilities and Services Near You
Main Address: 810 Vermont Ave. NW, Washington DC 20420
Toll Free: 1-800-827-1000
TTY: 1-800-829-4833
Forms: Department of Veterans Affairs Forms

Military OneSource:

https://www.militaryonesource.mil/: Military OneSource is a U.S. Department of Defense initiative that provides resources and assistance to active-duty, National Guard, and Reserve service members and their families all over the world, including those who are stationed overseas. Military OneSource is a 24-hour contact center and website that provides extensive information, referrals, and support on all aspects of military life and is available to all component members of the Armed Forces, as well as their families and survivors. There is a toll-free hotline (800) 342-9647. Military OneSource also provides access to confidential non-medical counseling for service members, their families, and survivors in the local community, as well as via telephone, secure online chat, and video. There are a variety of other services offered including tax preparation services in over 150 languages, financial planning advice, health and wellness consultations, and help for wounded warriors, among other services.

Ph: 800-342-9647 TTY/TDD: Dial 711;
email: wwrc@militaryonesource.com

Fort Thomas: Seven-Week PTSD Residential Program

https://www.va.gov/cincinnati-health-care/locations/cincinnati-va-medical-center-fort-thomas/

H. O. O. V. E. S.:

https://www.hooves.us/: A program for veterans with PTSD designed by a veteran, with one of the world's best programs for equine-assisted facilitation and stress-and-trauma coaching program. It is a non-profit, donor-supported group that runs free, four-day non-clinical retreats for military veterans and their families, as well as for first responder looking for help to alleviate the stress from their jobs.

4055 Wilkins Rd
Swanton, OH 43558
Phone: 419.930.7936
Email: info@hooves.us
EIN: 61-1609848

VA: National Center for PTSD

https://www.ptsd.va.gov/gethelp/peer_support.asp

Veterans Crisis Line:

1-800-273-8255 Press 1. Don't hesitate to get in touch with them whenever you need help.

Confidential Crisis Chat VeteransCrisisLine.net or text to 838255. They're always willing to listen to what you have to say.

Attorneys:

Jan Dils Attorneys at Law. Free consultations at 877 526-3457, website www.jandils.com for Social Security Disability support. Social Security Disability benefits may be available if you are unable to work because of a medical condition. Claiming disability benefits under the SSDI or SSI programs of the Social Security Administration can be complicated, as can the process of filing an application or appealing a decision. Some people have to wait for several years before they receive the disability benefits to which they are entitled. Disabled veterans across the country can speak to the legal team at Jan Dils, Attorneys at Law. Call them any time. Address:

963 Market St.
Parkersburg, WV 26101

Bergmann & Moore Attorneys at Law for veteran claims 877 838-2889. Former VA attorneys Glenn Bergmann and Joseph Moore lead this firm. Mr. Bergmann represented the VA before the U.S. Court of Appeals for Veterans Claims, and Mr. Moore wrote opinions for the VA Board of Veterans' Appeals in the Appellate Litigation Division. Since gaining insider knowledge of the VA, the two attorneys have devoted their time helping veterans and their families with VA compensation claims. Bergmann & Moore welcome veterans and their families to contact them at any time for a no-obligation consultation about their legal options. Intake coordinators are available to give you information, answer your questions, and point you to other resources. Address:

7920 Norfolk Avenue
Suite 700
Bethesda, MD 20814

Don't hesitate to get the help you need!

REFERENCES

Calming Trauma - How Understanding the Brain Can Help. (2019). Dawn McClelland. https://www.phoenix-society.org/resources/calming-trauma

Fight, Flight, Freeze, Fawn: Examining The 4 Trauma Responses. (2021, September 13). Mindbodygreen. https://www.mindbodygreen.com/articles/fight-flight-freeze-fawn-trauma-responses

The Basic Structure of Loss and Violence Trauma Imprints. (2020, June 3). Life. https://www.lifecenteredtherapy.com/post/the-basic-structure-of-loss-and-violence-trauma-imprints/

Psychiatry.org - What is Posttraumatic Stress Disorder (PTSD)? (2019). Felix Torres. https://www.psychiatry.org/patients-families/ptsd/what-is-ptsd

Hill & Ponton, P.A. (2021, May 11). *PTSD and Veterans: Breaking Down the Statistics*. https://www.hillandponton.com/veterans-statistics/ptsd/

Psych, B. D. (2020, December 1). *PTSD Examined: The Five Types of Post Traumatic Stress Disorder*. Best Day Psychiatry & Counseling. https://bestdaypsych.com/ptsd-examined-the-five-types-of-post-traumatic-stress-disorder/

Learn the Symptoms, Causes, and Treatment of PTSD. (2022, March 1). Verywell Mind. https://www.verywellmind.com/ptsd-in-the-dsm-5-2797324

Stanborough, R. M. J. (2021, July 7). *What Are the Treatment Options for PTSD?* Healthline. https://www.healthline.com/health/ptsd-treatment

ROBBINS RESEARCHINTERNATIONAL, INC. (2021, March 24). *How to use neuro-associative conditioning to transform your life*. Tonyrobbins.Com. https://www.tonyrobbins.com/personal-growth/neuro-associative-conditioning/

9 Ways to Relieve Anxiety Associated With PTSD. (2020, June 3). Verywell Mind. https://www.verywellmind.com/ways-of-coping-with-anxiety-2797619

How to Manage PTSD Stress With Stress Inoculation Training. (2021, August 12). Verywell Mind. https://www.verywellmind.com/stress-inoculation-training-2797682

Guideline, P. T. S. D. (2019). Treatments for PTSD. American Psychological Association. Retrieved April 25, 2022, from https://www.apa.org/ptsd-guideline/treatments

Ease the symptoms of PTSD with aromatherapy – PTSD UK. (2019). John. https://www.ptsduk.org/ease-symptoms-ptsd-aromatherapy/

REFERENCES

PTSD â Can Essential Oils Help Heal The Trauma? (2022). Amrita Aromatherapy. https://www.amrita.net/blog/essential-oils-for-post-traumatic-stress-disorder-ptsd

Equine Therapy Helps to Heal PTSD | NYP. (2020). Prudence Fisher. https://www.nyp.org/newsletters/prof-adv/psych/equine-therapy-helps-ptsd

Bucklin, S., & Young, A., MD. (2018, April 16). *PTSD Treatments and Therapies: Which Is Best for You?* EverydayHealth.Com. https://www.everydayhealth.com/ptsd/guide/treatment/

Is There a Cure for PTSD? (2021, July 1). Verywell Mind. https://www.verywellmind.com/ptsd-treatment-2797659

P.A., H. P. (2021, May 3). *Top 10 Tips for Supporting a Loved One with PTSD.* Hill & Ponton, P.A. https://www.hillandponton.com/top-10-tips-for-supporting-a-loved-one-with-ptsd/

M. (2022, March 16). *Helping Someone with PTSD.* HelpGuide.Org. https://www.helpguide.org/articles/ptsd-trauma/helping-someone-with-ptsd.htm

Planning for a mental health crisis. (2020). Mind. https://www.mind.org.uk/information-support/guides-to-support-and-services/crisis-services/planning-for-a-crisis/

Helping a Family Member Who Has PTSD | HealthLink BC. (2020). Healthwise Staff. https://www.healthlinkbc.ca/health-topics/helping-family-member-who-has-ptsd

GotQuestions.org. (2022, January 4). *What does the Bible say about PTSD?* https://www.gotquestions.org/Bible-PTSD.html

R. (2021, November 8). *What Would Jesus Say To Someone Struggling With PTSD?* REBOOT Recovery. https://rebootrecovery.com/what-would-jesus-say-ptsd/

Ministries, G. Q. (2020). What does the Bible say about recovering from PTSD? 412teens.Org. https://412teens.org/qna/what-does-the-Bible-say-about-recovering-from-PTSD.php

GotQuestions.org, G. Q. M. (2014, October 20). Home. GotQuestions.org. Retrieved April 25, 2022, from https://www.gotquestions.org/Bible-PTSD.html

Reyes, M. D. (2019, December 5). *A Christian Approach to Complex PTSD.* Seattle Christian Counseling. https://seattlechristiancounseling.com/articles/a-christian-approach-to-complex-ptsd

Fredrek, C. (2021, September 1). *3 Stages of Recovery from Trauma & PTSD in Therapy.* Healing Matters. https://healingmatters.ca/3-stages-of-recovery-from-trauma-ptsd-in-therapy/

Quirke, M. L. G. M. A. F. T. (2021, October 24). *Recovering from Complex PTSD: 3 Key Stages of Long-Term Healing.* Michael G. Quirke, MFT. https://michaelgquirke.com/recovering-from-complex-ptsd-3-key-stages-of-long-term-healing/

Bennett, T. (2020). *PTSD stages: What are the four phases of PTSD?* Thriveworks. https://thriveworks.com/blog/four-phases-ptsd-impact-rescue-intermediate-recovery-long-term-reconstruction/

Positivity, P. O. (2020, February 20). *8 Ways to Rebuild a Positive Life After Trauma | Power of Positivity.* Power of Positivity: Positive Thinking & Attitude. https://www.powerofpositivity.com/8-ways-to-rebuild-a-positive-life-after-trauma/

Greenberg, M. (2013). Turning to the positive: Personal growth after trauma ... Psychology Today. Retrieved April 25, 2022, from https://www.psychologytoday.com/us/blog/the-mindful-self-express/201303/turning-the-positive-personal-growth-after-trauma

P. (2019, July 24). *6 Ways To Pick Yourself Up After A Trauma.* Psychreg. https://www.psychreg.org/pick-yourself-up-after-a-trauma/

McAllister, B. J., MA. (2015, February 23). *Resensitization: Coming Back to Life after Trauma.* GoodTherapy.Org Therapy Blog. https://www.goodtherapy.org/blog/resensitization-coming-back-to-life-after-trauma-0223154

BrightQuest Treatment Centers. (2020, July 25). *PTSD Retraumatization -.* https://www.brightquest.com/post-traumatic-stress-disorder/retraumatization/

Raspolich, J. (2022, January 8). *What Is PTSD Retraumatization?* Vista Pines Health. https://vistapineshealth.com/services/ptsd-treatment/retraumatization/#:%7E:text=Retraumatization%20is%20the%20return%20of,traumatic%20event%20and%20PTSD%20symptoms

BrightQuest Treatment Centers. (2019, January 15). *Trauma, Retraumatization, and the Value of Long-Term PTSD Treatment.* https://www.brightquest.com/blog/trauma-re-traumatization-and-the-value-of-long-term-ptsd-treatment-centers/

VA.gov Home. (2019). Veterans Affairs. https://www.va.gov/

Military OneSource. (2022, April 22). *Support for Military Personnel & Families.* https://www.militaryonesource.mil/

Cincinnati VA Medical Center-Fort Thomas | VA Cincinnati health care. (2022, February 8). Veterans Affairs. https://www.va.gov/cincinnati-health-care/locations/cincinnati-va-medical-center-fort-thomas/

Serious male military reading bible, religion and faith, psychological therapy (2022) Available at:https://www.shutterstock.com/image-photo/serious-male-military-reading-bible-religion-1486344674 (Accessed: 15 May, 2022)

Mature psychologist smiling, shaking hands with middle aged military man after therapy session. Soldier suffering from depression, psychological trauma. PTSD concept. Focus on aged man (2022) Available at: https://www.shutterstock.com/image-photo/mature-psychologist-smiling-shaking-hands-middle-1785553226 (Accessed: 15 May, 2022)

Psychologist making notes during therapy session with sad male soldier, PTSD (2022) Available at:https://www.shutterstock.com/image-photo/psychologist-making-notes-during-therapy-session-1486344695 (Accessed: 15 May, 2022)

Special forces United States soldier or private military contractor with PTSD. Image on a black background (2022) Available at: https://www.shutterstock.com/image-photo/special-forces-united-states-soldier-private-1071658175 (Accessed: 15 May, 2022)

Portrait of young male and female soldier. Man and woman in military uniform on the war. Depressed and having problems with mental health and emotions, PTSD, rehabilitation. Creative collage (2022) Available at:https://www.shutterstock.com/image-photo/portrait-young-male-female-soldier-man-1397216378 (Accessed: 15 May, 2022)

Young Soldier Face with Jungle Camouflage Paint (2022) Available at: https://www.shutterstock.com/image-photo/young-soldier-face-jungle-camouflage-paint-82488826 (Accessed: 5 May, 2022)

A person walk into the misty foggy road in a dramatic mystic sunrise scene with abstract colors (2022) Available at:https://www.shutterstock.com/image-photo/person-walk-into-misty-foggy-road-163326239 (Accessed: 9 March, 2022)

Elite member of US Army rangers in combat helmet and dark glasses. Studio shot, dark black background, looking at camera, dark contrast (2022) Available at: https://www.shutterstock.com/image-photo/elite-member-us-army-rangers-combat-649292860 (Accessed: 9 March, 2022)

I hope you got value out of this book.

I'm very open to feedback and always looking to improve.

Could you maybe share your opinion of the book in a few words?

I'd love to know what you think and see if there are areas you are interested in that I have not covered.

PTSD Today

Https://googledocs.com/7 Little Known Ways to Help You Deal with

Made in the USA
Middletown, DE
26 April 2024